JOURNAL FOR THE STUDY OF THE OLD TESTAMENT
SUPPLEMENT SERIES
155

JSOT Press
Sheffield

Land Tenure and the Biblical Jubilee

Uncovering Hebrew Ethics through the Sociology of Knowledge

Jeffrey A. Fager

Journal for the Study of the Old Testament
Supplement Series 155

Copyright © 1993 Sheffield Academic Press

Published by JSOT Press
JSOT Press is an imprint of
Sheffield Academic Press Ltd
343 Fulwood Road
Sheffield S10 3BP
England

Typeset by Sheffield Academic Press
and
Printed on acid-free paper in Great Britain
by Biddles Ltd
Guildford

British Library Cataloguing in Publication Data

Fager, Jeffrey A.
    Land Tenure and the Biblical Jubilee: Uncovering Hebrew
    Ethics through the Sociology of Knowledge.—(JSOT
    Supplement Series, ISSN 0309-0787; No. 155)
    I. Title II. Series
    221.6

    ISBN 1-85075-398-9

CONTENTS

Part III
THE MORAL WORLD-VIEW OF THE JUBILEE

ABBREVIATIONS

AASOR	Annual of the American Schools of Oriental Research
ASTI	*Annual of the Swedish Theological Institute*
ATR	*Anglican Theological Review*
BA	*Biblical Archaeologist*
Bib	*Biblica*
BSO(A)S	*Bulletin of the School of Oriental (and African) Studies*
BTB	*Biblical Theology Bulletin*
BZ	*Biblische Zeitschrift*
CBC	Cambridge Bible Commentary
CBQ	*Catholic Biblical Quarterly*
EvT	*Evangelische Theologie*
HeyJ	*Heythrop Journal*
HUCA	*Hebrew Union College Annual*
IDBSup	*IDB*, Supplementary Volume
Int	*Interpretation*
JAOS	*Journal of the American Oriental Society*
JBL	*Journal of Biblical Literature*
JCS	*Journal of Cuneiform Studies*
JNES	*Journal of Near Eastern Studies*
JQR	*Jewish Quarterly Review*
JSOT	*Journal for the Study of the Old Testament*
JSS	*Journal of Semitic Studies*
JTS	*Journal of Theological Studies*
NRT	*La nouvelle revue théologique*
Or	*Orientalia*
OTL	Old Testament Library
PEQ	*Palestine Exploration Quarterly*
RB	*Revue biblique*
SBLDS	SBL Dissertation Series
SBLSP	SBL Seminar Papers
Scr	*Scripture*
VT	*Vetus Testamentum*
VTSup	*Vetus Testamentum*, Supplements
ZAW	*Zeitschrift für wissenschaftliche Theologie*

Part I

LAYING THE FOUNDATION

Chapter 1

THE USE OF THE SOCIOLOGY OF KNOWLEDGE IN EXAMINING THE JUBILEE

The legislation associated with the year of jubilee presents the most radical program for continuous social reform to be found in the Old Testament.[1] This is particularly the case with regard to land reform. Here the very basic notions of private property and economic viability are touched by a reform program that is quite thoroughgoing. The biblical jubilee presents a very rich resource for understanding the ancient Israelite moral world-view. Traditional exegetical methods, however, do not lead us to the deepest levels of meaning within this text. This study will rely on methods associated with the sociology of knowledge to examine carefully this legislation—how it came into being, why it was maintained and how it was used in a particular historical setting—thus providing a deeper understanding of the ethical implications of the jubilee.

A quick review of the history of interpretation of the jubilee indicates that, until very recently, nothing along these lines has been attempted. Ancient commentators gave their attention either to the fallow laws of the sabbath year or to the calculation of the jubilee cycles. By the time of these commentators there was no Israelite nation which had the power to enact laws regulating land tenure, and there was little pragmatic motivation to engender more careful reflection on the jubilee legislation dealing with land. With the Renaissance came an increased interest in the examination of many types of literature for which there were no immediately apparent practical applications. Typical of those early humanists was Peter van der Kun (1586–1638), who was also

---

1. A search of ancient Near Eastern legislation and royal decrees reveals no other case in which all land lost to a family is potentially subject to redistribution on a set, periodic basis (see J.A. Fager, 'Land Tenure and the Biblical Jubilee: A Moral World View' [Ann Arbor, MI: University Microfilms, 1987], pp. 25-45).

known as Petrus Cunaeus. Cunaeus believed that the Mosaic law was the outline for a perfect society ordained by God, in which the jubilee prevented inequalities of land distribution, thereby facilitating stability and morality by keeping the people 'industriously occupied in tilling their fields' and away from the decadence of the city.[1] This view of the jubilee relied on a straightforward understanding of the literal application of the law, although it confined such an observance to the Israelite nation and did not seek any deeper meaning lying under the surface of the regulations.

The major work done exclusively on the year of the jubilee in recent history is Robert North's *Sociology of the Biblical Jubilee*. This book built upon the work of the early humanists like Petrus Cunaeus and brought together a great deal of material on the historical and sociological data related to the year of the jubilee legislation. Yet the book focuses on the historical and sociological *realia* of the material and does not explain the socio-ethical foundations of the regulations—their *raison d'être*.

Since North's work, surprisingly little has been done on the year of the jubilee. Most of the literature has focused entirely on the historical data related to it or the direct application of jubilee principles to the modern social context in the West, but the latter essays have lacked careful exegetical analysis. Two notable exceptions are works by Robert Gnuse and Christopher J.H. Wright. They have used the results of previous study to determine the ancient Israelites' ethics toward the poor.[2] These are fine analyses; however, I believe a firmer foundation can be laid for an examination of the Israelite world-view by uncovering not only the origins of that world-view, but also the conscious and perhaps subconscious attitudes toward the moral life.

Most scholars agree that the land reform system described in Leviticus 25 was never put into practice.[3] But if that is correct, what

1. J.R. Ziskind, 'Petrus Cunaeus on Theocracy, Jubilee and the Latifundia', *JQR* 68 (1978), pp. 243-45.

2. R. Gnuse, *You Shall Not Steal: Community and Property in the Biblical Tradition* (Maryknoll, NY: Orbis Books, 1985); C.J.H. Wright, *God's People in God's Land: Family, Land, and Property in the Old Testament* (Grand Rapids: Eerdmans, 1990).

3. See the excursus below. Representative arguments can be found in R. Gnuse, 'Jubilee Legislation in Leviticus: Israel's Vision of Social Reform', *BTB* 15 (1985), pp. 43-48; J. van der Ploeg, 'Studies in Hebrew Law', *CBQ* 13 (1951), pp. 164-71; B.Z. Wacholder, 'The Calendar of Sabbatical Cycles during the Second Temple and

was its intent? Why did the concept of the year of the jubilee exist? Not only does that concept exist, it exists in a certain form—that of divine legislation—and it was used by certain people, namely, the priests. The land reform program of the year of the jubilee is put into the form of Mosaic law for a reason; there is a particular problem addressed by this legislation, and there is a particular solution presented for this problem. The land laws of Leviticus 25 are based on a system of land tenure and land reform, a system which was only one of several alternatives that could have been chosen. The reasons that underlie the movement and change in the jubilee tradition are part of a comprehensive understanding of the world and how people ought to live in it. To understand fully the ethics of the jubilee, one must understand the moral world-view upon which it is based.

In order to achieve this deeper meaning, we must turn to social world studies, which are based on methods developed within the social sciences. Compared to many of the other methods of biblical interpretation, social world studies represent newer forms of analysis for exegetes.[1] They have proved to be an important contribution to the way in which we examine ancient texts. The social sciences possess the advantage of having testable theories which can prevent the introduction of biases founded upon 'intuition'.[2] Unfortunately, outlining a strict social world methodology is nearly impossible. As James Flanagan states:

> Social world studies do not offer a single method or theory in the usual sense of the terms. Their dependence on standard biblical methodologies, archaeology, and comparative sociology make them derivative and eclectic in ways that defy methodological purity... Social world studies treat every society as unique, but the comparisons inject pragmatism, positivism, and Missouri style 'show-me-ism' that both expects and suspects consistencies in human behavior.[3]

The use of social world studies is based on a certain assumption about

---

the Early Rabbinic Period', *HUCA* 44 (1973), pp. 153-96; and R. Westbrook, 'Jubilee Laws', *Israel Law Review* 6 (1971), pp. 209-26.

1.   For a concise summary of the development of social world studies on the Bible, see J.W. Flanagan, *David's Social Drama: A Hologram of Israel's Early Iron Age* (The Social World of Biblical Antiquities Series, 7; Sheffield: Almond Press, 1988), pp. 53-72.

2.   B.J. Malina, 'The Social Sciences and Biblical Interpretation', *Int* 36, p. 240.

3.   Flanagan, *David's Social Drama*, pp. 53-72.

how texts communicate their meanings. Bruce Malina helpfully summarized how the social sciences improve a reader's ability to comprehend texts which particular social systems might produce.[1] A text is not a series of propositions organized according to a deep structure by which anyone knowing the vocabulary and the rules of grammar and syntax will understand the text's meaning. Rather, a text is a 'scenario'. Readers couple scenes or schemes from the text with settings, episodes or models which already exist in their minds and are derived from their own experience. While the text may provide certain alterations to those settings, episodes or models, the author uses a familiar 'domain of reference', or social world, to evoke more or less predictable responses. Knowledge of the original reader's domain of reference is necessary in order to understand the meaning intended within the text.[2]

Social scientists help provide such knowledge. Specifically, they have developed three models to describe a social world.[3] First, the structural functionalist model views society as a static system in which every element has a function in maintaining the integrity of society. These social elements are based on a 'consensus of values' among the population, and any change that does not function to maintain the system is considered 'deviant'. Secondly, the conflict model assumes society is an aggregate of groups competing to attain their own goals, with the stronger groups coercing others to acquiesce. In this case change and conflict are the normal state of affairs. Thirdly, the symbolic model analyzes society by examining the symbolic meaning which society attaches to valued objects in the world and by determining how society organizes and interprets the world in light of those symbolic meanings. Each of the three models contributes to a complete understanding of a social world since each provides its own important insight into the way societies exist.

The present study of the jubilee will incorporate all three of these models. I will examine how land tenure laws functioned to maintain a stable economic environment and how the priestly group[4] adapted the jubilee to recreate a stability which had been lost. The priestly group,

1. Malina, 'The Social Sciences and Biblical Interpretation'.
2. Malina, 'The Social Sciences and Biblical Interpretation'.
3. Malina, 'The Social Sciences and Biblical Interpretation', pp. 233-36.
4. For the purpose of this study, I will focus on the priestly group which formulated the jubilee legislation in the late exilic period.

however, was not the only one seeking stability; an 'Ezekielian school' was in competition with the priests to redefine society. An examination of that conflict—that is, the contrast between the priests' and the Ezekielians' alternative definitions of land reform—aids our knowledge of their models of an ideal social world. I will use the sociology of knowledge to uncover and examine these models.

The sociology of knowledge provides the tool of inquiry which will enable us to formulate hypotheses regarding this text. It is based upon the proposition (rooted in the thought of Karl Marx) that social location affects one's perspective, which in turn determines the meaning of objects—including language.[1] While strict Marxian historical materialism has come under critical scrutiny by recent social scientists who recognize that humans play a more active role in shaping society and religion than some (e.g. Gottwald) have suggested,[2] the sociology of knowledge assumes a dialectic relationship between individuals and society. After an examination of the history of the jubilee tradition and of a group of priests who adopted that tradition in the late exilic period, I will use the sociology of knowledge to illuminate the ways in which the priests' social location affected their adoption of what they received from their predecessors, and then determine how the priests constructed an orderly world and the connection between that world and their moral system.

How are we to understand the constitution of a 'world', and what does that mean for this case? Human existence is characterized by a basic openness within the world. That is, humans have little intrinsic (genetic) guidance for thinking—unlike other animals, whose instincts control their mental activity and 'give' them an ordered world. Therefore, people have produced their own order (society) which organizes thought and keeps existence from dissolving into chaos.[3] It

---

1. K. Mannheim, *Ideology and Utopia: An Introduction to the Sociology of Knowledge* (trans. L. Wirth and E. Shils; New York: Harcourt Brace Jovanovich, 1936), pp. 264-73; P.L.Berger and T. Luckmann, *The Social Construction of Reality: A Treatise in the Sociology of Knowledge* (Garden City, NY: Doubleday, 1966), pp. 5-7.

2. This caveat, along with several others regarding the use of the social sciences for biblical studies, is found in G.A. Herion, 'The Impact of Modern and Social Science Assumptions on the Reconstruction of Israelite History', *JSOT* 34 (1986), pp. 3-33.

3. Berger and Luckmann, *The Social Construction of Reality*, pp. 45-50; and C. Geertz, *The Interpretation of Culture: Selected Essays* (New York: Basic Books, 1973), pp. 217-18.

is a biological necessity that humans externalize their subjective consciousness in order to make a world which then becomes objectively real and finally is internalized by them into their subjective consciousness.[1] That is to say, the construction of an orderly world is a dialectic process which has three movements; (1) humans produce society, (2) society is considered to be an objective reality and (3) society molds humans.[2] The task of world building is actually a task of ordering or classifying the objects and events observed in the flux of experience into a coherent and comprehensible structure.[3] All humans participate in this dialectic process whereby the world becomes predictable and, thus, habitable. The priests were also engaged in this human process of ordering, maintaining and reforming the world which their predecessors had handed on to them.

Once a world is created, the objects of that world, either material (e.g. tools) or nonmaterial (e.g. language), take on existence independent of the absolute control of their creator, humanity, and thus become objective and shareable.[4] As these objects are shared within a society, meanings are attributed to them, and those meanings become a taken-for-granted knowledge which is then mediated throughout the society and to the next generation.[5] (In this book, the example of such knowledge is the 'jubilee tradition'.) However, since the creation and maintenance of a world constitute a dialectic process, in which people influence the social world as well as being shaped by it, there is always the tendency for people to attribute new meanings to familiar objects. After all, every individual, generation and societal subgroup views the world from its own particular perspective—either slightly or significantly different from others. If that tendency were allowed to be actualized without restraint, an orderly world could not be maintained long enough to provide any stability. Therefore, every society must have a social base which provides the processes and institutions

1. P.L. Berger, *The Sacred Canopy: Elements of a Sociological Theory of Religion* (Garden City, NY: Doubleday, 1967; Anchor Books, 1969), pp. 4-5.

2. Berger and Luckmann, *The Social Construction of Reality*, pp. 50-63.

3. Berger, *The Sacred Canopy*, pp. 19-20.

4. Berger, *The Sacred Canopy*, pp. 9-10.

5. See H.L. Harrod, *The Human Center: Moral Agency in the Social World* (Philadelphia: Fortress Press, 1981), pp. 32-33.

that are able to provide legitimation for the social order.[1] These processes and institutions provide the social forces which keep individual interpretations of the world within acceptable bounds. (By definition they are 'conservative' in that they tend to conserve the social order.) If that base is weakened or destroyed, the shared meanings that constitute the social world change, resulting in the formation of a new world.[2] Throughout Israel's history, its social structure underwent many changes. One example was the shift from a loose confederation to a centralized monarchy. It seems that the taken-for-granted notion of 'jubilee' survived—but in a different form. The Babylonian exile represented a catastrophic disruption in the society's plausibility structure, and the frenzy of literary activity in that period can be construed as an attempt to recreate a viable world. Again, the jubilee was caught in this whirlpool of change.

Societies also share meanings that transcend the everyday world, meanings related to abstractions or concepts which are not experienced normally in a person's day to day activity. In order to mediate those meanings a society requires symbols—everyday objects, persons or events which are 'paired with meanings that transcend the everyday world'.[3] Clifford Geertz adds that symbols are not only shaped by reality, but they also shape reality.[4] Again, we see a dialectic process in which humans both create the methods of mediating the meanings of the social world and are shaped by those methods of mediation. Thus, as the priests refine a legal code for the purpose of creating a social base to support the world which they must rebuild, they are also influenced by the symbolic meanings they have been given by the preceding generation. Both sides of the dialectic are significant in understanding the full import of their ethical pronouncements.

Religion was certainly an important transcendent reality for Israel (and the vast majority of cultures throughout history) and the one within which the jubilee was finally placed. Berger defines religion as 'the establishment, through human activity, of an all-embracing sacred order, that is, of a sacred cosmos that will be capable of maintaining

1.   Berger, *The Sacred Canopy*, p. 45.

2.   See Harrod, *The Human Center*, p. 115.

3.   Harrod, *The Human Center*, p. 19; note also Berger and Luckmann, *The Social Construction of Reality*, p. 38

4.   Geertz, *The Interpretation of Cultures*, pp. 91-94.

itself in the ever-present face of chaos'.[1] The priests were trying to explain the universe in terms of an order that participated in the stability and power of the divine, an order that could be relied upon to exist in the future, thus allowing the people to live with hope in a seemingly uncertain present. The legal system they devised, with all its ritual, was a means of reinforcing the symbolic (religious) meanings that supported their world.[2]

Once a universe is understood, it is possible to know how to live in it because there is a continuity between the descriptive (what is) and the normative (what ought to be) in universe construction and maintenance.[3] Geertz has examined this continuity and discovered that sacred symbols lie at the connection between a society's 'is' and its 'ought'. Since humans create sacred symbols in order to structure an otherwise chaotic world, these symbols can function to describe how the universe actually exists and to explain the natural ethos of that world, that is, the moral and aesthetic qualities that would naturally characterize a people who lived in such a universe. The metaphysical reality of the world and the social ethics of a community reinforce each other; what ought to be tends to be seen as what actually is, and what actually is tends to be proclaimed as what ought to be.[4] This same continuity is to be found throughout the Old Testament, and it is quite pronounced in the priestly work. The priests clearly connected a particular cosmic order with a particular style of behavior, each implying the other to the point that to deny one meant to deny the other. The cult in all its complexity was given by God as a means of maintaining order in the universe, and any neglect of the cult resulted in the breakdown of that order.

Of course, when the reality of the world undergoes a major change, the 'ought' and the 'is' no longer correspond, and a society is threatened with moral chaos as well as social disruption. That is, as the social institutions which had legitimated the social order on the basis of a cosmic order fall, people lose confidence in the very cosmic order that presumably upheld the society. That leads to a questioning of all normative systems associated with the 'faltering' cosmic order. Those responsible for the maintenance of a society must not only explain

1. Berger, *The Sacred Canopy*, p. 51.
2. See Harrod, *The Human Center*, p. 134.
3. Berger and Luckmann, *The Social Construction of Reality*, p. 101.
4. See Geertz, *The Interpretation of Cultures*, pp. 89-127.

why the disruption occurred in the first place, but they must also recreate a world that can command the confidence of the community. Berger and Luckmann describe four stages in this process of legitimation; (1) passing along what is considered 'objective reality', (2) supporting that reality with rudimentary theoretical propositions, (3) developing explicit theories created by specialists handling specific fields of knowledge, and (4) constructing a symbolic universe.[1] At least three of these stages were present during the exile. The objective meanings shared by the Israelite community—represented by the priestly view[2]—were gathered and written down for the purpose of transmitting them to a new generation, insofar as those shared meanings retained viability after the fall of Jerusalem. Those who gathered the traditions added theoretical reasons for the exile, specifically, disobedience to the Yahwistic law that maintained the former world. The priests were certainly a group of specialists dealing with the specific knowledge (cultic matters) who systemized the material in light of a particular notion of the world. The fourth stage, an explicit explication of the symbolic universe, is not readily apparent within the text since the priests did not function as systematic theologians. Indeed, very few texts display, in any direct way, the symbolic universe upon which they rest. This study will attempt to discover the universe which lies behind the jubilee.

More specifically, I will attempt to discover the moral world-view that lies behind the jubilee. From what has already been said concerning the continuity between the 'ought' and the 'is', it is clear that a 'moral' world-view cannot be separated from the more general understanding of the world as a whole. However, there are certain aspects of a 'moral' world-view that give it special characteristics which ought to be noted. Morality is a way of apprehending the world in terms of 'a realm of value meanings'.[3] While value meanings transcend the everyday world of human finitude and embodiment, they are related to experiences of objects of the everyday world, and a community's

---

1.　Berger and Luckmann, *The Social Construction of Reality*, pp. 87-88.

2.　How widely the Israelite community shared particular meanings like the jubilee is difficult to determine. The adoption of Mesopotamian land laws by premonarchic Israel *might* suggest a broad knowledge of a basic concept of an agrarian society. Even if that is the case, the concept of jubilee might have become an esoteric idea shared only by the intelligentsia.

3.　Harrod, *The Human Center*, p. 5.

symbols must maintain that relation in order to bond daily activity to the deeper sensibilities of value.[1] A moral world-view encompasses those symbols that organize the value meanings into a system that coherently directs behavior in the community, providing individuals with the motivation to act according to the shared value meanings of the community. The priests had a certain moral world-view which organized the value meanings they received from their predecessors and formed the foundation of the jubilee. To understand that moral world-view is to understand the ethics of the jubilee.

Mannheim's Three Levels of Meaning

In his foundational essay on world-view, Mannheim described three levels of meaning for any social phenomenon.[2] These three levels are divisible only for analytic purposes, but in so doing it is easier to see the deeper levels of a world-view expressed in an act or institution. Therefore, Part III of this study will conduct such an analysis in order to explore the underlying moral world-view of the jubilee. The first level of meaning is the 'objective meaning'.[3] At this level, one is dealing with the bare sociological data of a phenomenon. If one is dealing with an act, this level refers to the events that occurred, events available to the senses, for example, the actual events one might observe at a baseball game or a cocktail party (who attended, what was served, the content of the conversation). If one is dealing with an institution (like the jubilee), this refers to the actual structure and rules of the institution as we find it in Leviticus 25 and the real effects of its existence.

The second level of meaning is the 'expressive meaning'. This level refers to the intent of the actors involved in the social phenomenon. Different individuals or groups may intend to express very different meanings by performing the same act or participating in the same institution. Baseball players may intend to express the virtue of com-

---

1.   Harrod, *The Human Center*, pp. 43-44, 67.

2.   K. Mannheim, 'On the Interpretation of *Weltanshauung*', in P. Kecskemeti (ed.), *Essays on the Sociology of Knowledge* (New York: Oxford University Press, 1952), pp. 44-46.

3.   I have retained Mannheim's label even though true objectivity may be unattainable; even the most 'obvious' facts are filtered through subjective perceptions. Nevertheless, this level represents those aspects of a phenomenon that are most available to independent scrutiny, minimizing distortion.

petition, the necessity of being a winner, or the desire to entertain by playing the game. Politicians may intend to express the importance of justice, the superiority of representative governance, or the drive for power by becoming involved in the legislative process. In the case of the jubilee, we will be examining the intent of priests in their adoption and redaction of the jubilee tradition. The expressive meaning is more subtle, and we must investigate several clues that will aid in the search for the priests' intent, clues that include the social location of the priests, the jubilee laws that do not deal with land tenure, the form and the concept of divine ownership.

However, every social phenomenon carries a meaning that is distinguishable from the surface level facts and the intent of the actors; Mannheim refers to this level as the 'documentary meaning'. The very existence of the game of baseball or the very existence of a constitutional republic implies a world-view that gives birth to such events or institutions. This world-view is so basic to a society's way of existing that few people are conscious of its existence even though their lives are guided by it. Regardless of the priests' intent in formulating the jubilee as they did, the jubilee carries its own meaning which is based on that underlying world-view. The documentary meaning is not totally independent from the objective or expressive levels. The existence of capital punishment may result from a world-view in which there is a relatively low regard for life (in that the state sanctions the taking of it) or a relatively high regard for life (in that the taking of it exacts the ultimate penalty). However, capital punishment would not result from a world-view in which there was no regard for life at all.

Again it must be emphasized that these levels may be separated for analytical purposes only; they function simultaneously and dialectically. The objective meaning is limited by the world-view, and the actor's intent is informed by it. On the other hand, actors may begin to reinterpret objective meaning, and, thus, shift the world-view. So my analysis will involve all three levels, understanding why this particular institution (with its own structure and rules) was used by these particular priests. After such a study, I will then describe the moral world-view of the jubilee.

The ultimate goal of this study is the successful use of a method which can provide a deeper understanding of the ethics of the Old

Testament.[1] It is an attempt to go beyond a description of what was and to probe the deeper motivations of what was. Whereas philosophy attempts to answer the great ontological and epistemological questions, the sociology of knowledge seeks to understand why this or that society gives the particular ontological and epistemological answers it does.[2] Thus, I will highlight certain basic understandings which some Israelites had of their world and how those understandings resulted in the institution of the jubilee.

1.   It is my hope that this method might aid in appropriating the message of the text for the modern world, but that is another step not within the purview of this book.

2.   Berger and Luckmann, *The Social Construction of Reality*, pp. 2-3.

Chapter 2

THE HISTORICAL BACKGROUND OF THE JUBILEE

While this is a study of the moral world-view and not a traditio-historical analysis of the development of an idea or a text, the historical background of the biblical jubilee cannot be ignored. Understanding any world-view requires a study of its history—where it came from, and how it developed.[1]

In the process, I will use Peter Dorner's definition of land tenure:

> Land tenure institutions constitute the legal and contractual or customary arrangements whereby people in farming gain access to productive opportunities on the land. These tenure arrangements determine the ability of individuals to gain access to these opportunities, and define in part the nature, dimensions and future security of such opportunities. In short, land tenure institutions determine the pattern of income distribution in the farm sector.[2]

As can be seen from this definition, the issue of actual ownership may or may not play a role; the central issue is access, that is, who receives the benefit of the productivity of certain parcels of land. In the case of the jubilee legislation, literal ownership does play a role in access to the land, but in a way far different from that of the modern Western world. (That difference is discussed in Part III.) In addition, the term

---

1. In effect, this would call for a diachronic study as well as a synchronic one. John Barton recommends this procedure for attaining the most accurate description of an ethical stance in ancient Israel. See J. Barton, 'Understanding Old Testament Ethics', *JSOT* 9 (1978), pp. 44-64. For the purposes of this analysis, the synchronic study comprises the bulk of the book, but the diachronic approach has not been ignored. For a much fuller investigation of the history of the concept of the jubilee and the development of the jubilee law, see Fager, 'Land Tenure and the Biblical Jubilee'.

2. P. Dorner, 'Land Tenure Institutions', in *Institutions in Agricultural Development* (Ames: Iowa State University Press, 1971), p. 15.

'land reform' will be used frequently when referring to the jubilee. Here land reform refers to the redistribution of land (or access to the land) in order to conform to the traditionally accepted beliefs about land tenure. That is to say, land reform is an institution whereby the socially accepted land tenure arrangements are restored after they have been disrupted.

In the Ancient Near East

The purpose of this summary is to understand the roots of the idea that led to the jubilee legislation. For some years it seemed that scholars assumed either that Israel borrowed stories, customs and laws directly from other ancient Near Eastern cultures or that Israel arrived in Palestine as a unique culture, untainted by outside influences. It is much more likely that Israel was a part of the greater ancient Near Eastern context and that Israel filtered, adapted or recreated foreign ideas to conform to its own particular social needs. Therefore, the land tenure and land reform institutions of the other ancient Near Eastern societies may have been known by Israel and adapted insofar as they proved congruent with and useful to Israel's traditional beliefs. In addition, aspects of a basic world-view remain within these laws in spite of the intent of those adopting them. Thus, when Mesopotamian land laws are known, one can gain a better view of those early notions in the greater ancient Near Eastern milieu that culminated in the Israelite jubilee.

It is clear that, even though land tenure in the ancient Near East was quite complex, there are a few aspects of it that appear frequently among the many cultures which have been studied, and these aspects provide fertile ground in which the Israelite jubilee could grow.[1] First, kings often proclaimed a 'release' that included the manumission of slaves, the cancellation of debts and the return of lost land. How often or with what regularity such edicts were proclaimed is still unknown, and there is no evidence that they occurred with the automatic regularity called for by the biblical jubilee. However, such edicts do introduce the concept of 'release' whereby what is perceived as an unjust distribution of wealth can be rectified. (At least, the kings presented these decrees as examples of their justice.) Secondly, a separation is

---

1. For an examination of particular examples of land tenure systems in the ancient Near East, see Fager, 'Land Tenure and the Biblical Jubilee', pp. 25-45.

often made between land ownership and the right to a land's produce. For example, in Assyria, land could be leased for a specified amount of time, allowing the owner to retain possession of the land while the lessee received the usufruct.[1] This distinction between ownership and access allowed the possibility of a poor landowner to take advantage of the equity in the land without losing the land permanently—a concept crucial to the jubilee, as it, too, allows the usufruct to be used in obtaining liquid assets. Thirdly, many of the systems presupposed the inalienability of land outside the family and created 'quasi-adoptions' in order to circumvent that prohibition. This concept of an inalienable patrimony is found frequently in the Hebrew Bible and is foundational for the jubilee. Finally, and most importantly, all these ancient Near Eastern regulations concerning land tenure set limits on individuals' rights to buy and sell land at will. There is a common recognition that land is such an essential ingredient in the survival of the people that the absolute right of use and disposal entails a great deal of power. Therefore, all these societies set boundaries around this power (which was then often concentrated in the monarchy), making land something quite different from other commodities, whose ownership was not as crucial for economic security.

Any examination of ancient Near Eastern land tenure must cover many different societies in a broad geographical area, and therefore conclusions concerning any diachronic progression will be general. With that disclaimer, two movements do seem to appear. First, there is a centralization of control of the land from smaller social units (families and tribes) to the monarchy. Many of the regulations of the ancient kingdoms presuppose land tenure systems based on family ownership and control of the land, but in those empires which absorbed tribal societies, a system of centralized authority in controlling land tenure was imposed upon the older tribal controls. Secondly, there is a movement toward greater rights of private owners of the land. In the case of family ownership and the inalienability of family land, the 'quasi-adoptions' became a means to sell the land permanently, thus giving the individual the absolute right of disposal. It may also be observed that after time, royal lands granted to particular persons became independent of the crown and were bought and sold as private land.

---

1. R. Clay, *The Tenure of Land in Babylonia and Assyria* (University of London Institute of Archaeology, Occasional Paper 1; London: The Institute, 1938), p. 20.

Thus we can see a tension within the attitudes toward land tenure in the ancient Near East. On the one hand, there was the recognition that land was a special resource that must receive special regulation in order to prevent the ruin of the people. On the other hand, there was a movement toward greater individual freedom in the use and disposal of the land, allowing for the possibility of latifundism and the pauperization of masses of people. It appears that the ancient Near East was pulled in the latter direction, and it was in such a context in which Israel came into being. Direct dependence on any of the systems described above is unlikely; however, the people of Israel were not isolated from the forces of the ancient Near Eastern milieu, so that the features and movements within the system of land tenure would have influenced—positively or negatively—Israel's formation of a land tenure policy.

In Early Israel

Without attempting an exhaustive study of premonarchic Israel, it is possible to determine that particular beliefs about land tenure were handed down to subsequent generations, who produced the jubilee. Discovering roots for the jubilee in Israel's early period not only indicates the tenacity with which such views of land tenure were held, but it also supports the thesis that the jubilee deliberately used ancient traditions as a stabilizing factor in a period of crisis.

Tribal Ethics
In H. Eberhard von Waldow's study of social responsibility in ancient Israel, he finds the roots of such responsibility in the tribal ethics the Israelites brought into Canaan.[1] In particular, he believes that the apodictic ordinances protecting the poor (the widow, orphan and sojourner)

---

1. H.E. von Waldow, 'Social Responsibility and Social Structure in Early Israel', *CBQ* 32 (1970), pp. 185-89. Even if Gottwald is correct in calling into question the tribal nature of the 'first' Israelites, at the time of their revolt from the Canaanite overlords, the newly liberated peasants formed a 'retribalised' confederation and would have 'reappropriated' the tribal ethics described by von Waldow. That is to say, they adopted a tribal heritage through their acceptance of the patriarchal narratives as their own and formed a 'tribal ethos' based upon that projected heritage. (See N.K. Gottwald, *The Tribes of Yahweh: A Sociology of the Religion of Liberated Israel, 1250–1050 BCE* [New York: Orbis Books, 1979].)

were rooted in the tribal life of the Semites before the establishment of
states. The social order was founded on unwritten laws of a general
ethos within kinship associations 'which were transmitted and enforced
by the *pater-familias*'.[1] Such a community shared status and wealth or
poverty; therefore, private property could not accumulate with a few
individuals to the detriment of some members of the community—
even the vulnerable members such as widows, orphans or sojourners.
In the formation of Israel itself, these ordinances never became part
of the civil law, but they were incorporated into the covenant between
Yahweh and the cultic community, a covenant renewed every seven
years. With all this, von Waldow hypothesizes a scenario whereby the
clans occupied and cleared land for agriculture, the land was surveyed
according to the number of families in the clan, and the families
received equal shares of the land by allotment, thus creating parity at
the family level which was the basic economic unit.[2] Such a scenario is
quite speculative, but the basic tribal world-view that would make
such a system possible was present.

Once such land was allotted to a family, it became a part of the
patrimony of that family from generation to generation. Again, this
concept of patrimony is rooted in the structure of the patriarchal–
tribal society, which explains its presence at Mari and Nuzi and its
absence in the Mesopotamian societies.[3] In his commentary on
Leviticus, J.R. Porter argues that the original jubilee law was based
on ancient land tenure systems in which the family held property and
no individual member of the family had the right to sell it.[4] Since the
patrimony belonged to the whole family and since the economic
security of the whole family was dependent upon the retention of that
patrimony, the whole family must be a part of any decision to sell it.
(One can note Abraham's purchase of the cave of Machpelah as an
example of this concept. [Gen. 23.3-16].) Porter also notes that this
ancient law of family property dealt only with agricultural land since
walled cities were foreign to the culture; therefore, the jubilee

---

1.   Von Waldow, 'Social Responsibility', p. 186.
2.   Von Waldow, 'Social Responsibility', p. 193.
3.   A. Malamat, 'Mari and the Bible: Some Patterns of Tribal Organizations and
Institutions', *JAOS* 82 (1962), p. 150.
4.   J.R. Porter, *Leviticus* (CBC; Cambridge: Cambridge University Press, 1976),
p. 201.

legislation could pass off houses in walled cities as private property.[1] Paul Hanson admits the great difficulty in sketching a 'complete history' of the concept of patrimony (*naḥalâ*) in ancient Israel, but his study leads him to conclude that 'the tribes of Benjamin and Joseph likely subscribed to the idea of an even-handed distribution of land as a part of their understanding of covenant'.[2]

This apparent correspondence between the jubilee and ancient tribal ethics suggests the possibility that attitudes toward the land which are reflected in the jubilee reach back to the very beginning of Israel. (I will discuss these attitudes in detail in Part III.) Anton Jirku believes that the patriarchalism, the solidarity of the people, and the emphasis on tribes within the jubilee concept prove that some notion of the jubilee 'was accepted into Israel soon after the migration into Palestine'.[3] In addition, Stephen Bess considers it 'scarcely conceivable' that certain jubilee concepts (like the inalienability of real estate) could have arisen during the monarchy or later.[4] Whether there were literal legal provisions resembling the jubilee legislation as it exists in Leviticus 25 or not, the beliefs about land tenure that lead naturally to such legislation seem to have existed from Israel's beginnings. Von Waldow argues that with such beliefs the newly settled Israel was an egalitarian society that made no provisions for private land ownership while all have a secure share in the land.[5] Caution must be taken in making such an assertion; certainly, by the time of Saul, some social stratification had occurred, and the traditions about the period of the judges indicate some economic inequality. However, present evidence indicates that the radical stratification that leads to a bimodal society did not take place until after the establishment of the monarchy.

Economic Factors

As well as arguments based on correspondence with tribal ethics,

---

1.　Porter, *Leviticus*, p. 202.

2.　P.D. Hanson, *The People Called: The Growth of a Community in the Bible* (San Francisco: Harper & Row, 1986), pp. 33-34, 65.

3.　A. Jirku, 'Das Israelitische Jobeljahr', in *Von Jerusalem nach Ugarit* (Graz, Austria: Akademische Druck- u. Verlagsanstalt, 1966), pp. 319-29 (328).

4.　S. Bess, 'Systems of Land Tenure in Ancient Israel' (dissertation, University of Michigan, 1963), p. 118 n. 178. See also W. Brueggemann, 'The Kerygma of the Priestly Writers', in W. Brueggemann and H. Walther Wolff (eds.), *Vitality of Old Testament Traditions* (Atlanta: John Knox, 1975), p. 107.

5.　Von Waldow, 'Social Responsibility', p. 194.

economic factors also argue for the early roots of the jubilee. North
believes that the *Sitz im Leben* is better understood as the period of
occupation, when hopes for growth were so high that restrictions
were required, rather than the period of restoration.[1] This assumes
that the restrictions recognized that the temptations of the new land
would lead some to attempt land acquisition at the expense of weaker
members of the community. By itself, this argument holds for any
period of prosperity in which there is sufficient venture capital available and sufficient confidence in the future of the economy to invest
that capital. Albrecht Alt adds to this the explanation that a redistribution of agricultural land by lottery 'is a procedure often found among
semi-nomads'.[2] Parallel to this is his argument that the practice of the
fallow year must have appeared before the Israelites had settled into
an agrarian life style, when a universal fallow would not have been
economically feasible.[3] However, Alt's comments about land redistribution are based on outdated methods of comparative analysis,[4] and it
is not at all clear that the fallow laws were intended to be observed
universally. In addition, David Hopkins has provided a reasonable
explanation of how a universal fallow could have been observed.[5]

A more convincing economic argument for the early roots of the
jubilee is one based on its regularity. Throughout the ancient Near
East there was the recognition that occasionally a 'release' needed to be
declared in order to prevent an economic crisis that might cause the
collapse of the society. However, such a decree always came from a
king; therefore, in a community without a king, an alternative system
would have been responsible for those occasional releases. Thus, the
set regularity of the jubilee was the Israelites' way of providing

---

1. R. North, *Sociology of the Biblical Jubilee* (Rome: Pontifical Biblical
Institute, 1954), pp. 204-205. Bess also believes that 'the statement of Lev. 25.23
was not given to justify change, but to forestall it' ('Land Tenure', p. 85).

2. A. Alt, 'The Origins of Israelite Law', in *Essays on Old Testament History
and Religion* (trans. R.A. Wilson; Garden City, NY: Doubleday, 1967), p. 166
n. 119.

3. Alt, 'The Origins of Israelite Law', p. 165 n. 118.

4. Alt bases his thesis on the work of Musil in *Arabia Petraea* and Schaeffer in
Hebrew Tribal Economy and the Jubilee.

5. D.C. Hopkins, *The Highlands of Canaan: Agricultural Life in the Early Iron
Age* (The Social World of Biblical Antiquity Series, 3; Sheffield: Almond Press,
1985), pp. 191-202.

economic reform in the absence of a king.[1] Indeed, Bess argues that the fixed intervals of the jubilee years stabilized the economy insofar as they removed the uncertainty of the accession of a new king.[2] One could depend on the arrival of a jubilee at certain intervals and make economic plans accordingly. In addition, even though the premonarchic economy was quite different from the commercial monarchy, it had its own complexities that required regulation that would have kept it well ordered.[3] All of this still does not prove that a regular economic reform based on ancient concepts of family-based land tenure (that is, at least a precursor of the jubilee if not the jubilee itself) was a part of premonarchic Israel, but it does show that premonarchic Israel did provide the proper environment for such a reform.

Theological Factors

It also appears that the theological reason given for the jubilee, namely, the divine ownership of the land, is also ancient. Lev. 25.23 echoes an old concept borrowed from Israel's neighbors that the deity was the owner of the land and the people were sojourners in it.[4] Hyacinthe-M. Dion even goes so far as to say that Yahweh is actually the name of a resident god of Canaan upon whose land the Hebrews moved.[5] William Robertson Smith's work, although somewhat outdated at many points, still provides interesting insights into this notion. Divine ownership was related to the land's agricultural function and, thus, to its fecundity. Land rendered fertile through human efforts (irrigation for example) was human property, but land rendered fertile by divine activity was divine property, and people lived on it at the pleasure of the deity. (Note Deut. 11.10-12 for a later description of Canaan as such a land.) There came to be a correspondence between a god's land and his people, so that whoever dwelt on the god's land was his people, and wherever his people dwelt was his land. With regard to the Israelites, the relationship of the people to Yahweh changed from kin status, an inherited and secure relationship, to client status—a dependency upon

---

1.   J. Lewy, 'The Biblical Institution of *Derôr*' in the Light of Akkadian Documents', *Eretz Israel* 5 (1958), p. 29.

2.   Bess, 'Land Tenure', p. 140.

3.   Bess, 'Land Tenure', pp. 144-46.

4.   H.-M. Dion, 'Yahweh, Dieu de Canaan, et la terre des hommes', *Canadian Journal of Theology* 13 (1967), pp. 233-34.

5.   Dion, 'Yahweh, Dieu de Canaan', pp. 235-40.

the bounty of God, a status which was maintained by obedience to the deity.[1] This change occurred very early, as the idea that Canaan belonged to Yahweh was taken up into the tribal confederation at the very beginning of Israel's existence.[2]

Important in the life of the confederation were the festivals at which the community celebrated that which brought them together, and it is possible that the jubilee also has roots in at least one of these festivals. Alt claims that every seventh year, the apodictic law was recited at the Feast of Tabernacles, the autumnal new year festival which celebrated new beginning in life. That entire seventh year was a year of rest in which the people sacrificed their right to the usufruct of the land to reaffirm 'the true and sole ownership of Yahweh'.[3] Lemche notes the possible connection between the '*mûk*-laws' of Lev. 25.39-54 and the manumission laws found in Exodus 21 and Deuteronomy 15, and then asserts that if 'jubilee' refers to 'release' (as North convincingly argues), it may have originally referred to a seven-year term.[4] Given the nature of the Feast of Tabernacles, part of the process of covenant renewal would have been the reaffirmation of the reception of the land from Yahweh and possibly the reallocation of that land to the tribes, clans and families.[5] Alt believes that the jubilee legislation was originally intended for every sabbatical year but was transformed to every seventh seven-year cycle (or every fifty years) 'after the complete transition of the people to an agricultural economy had made it impossible to carry out the original commandment'.[6] This cultic setting for jubilee concepts would have reinforced the theological foundations for the ancient land tenure system and provided a ritualistic expression of what was considered to be reality.

Some comment is needed on the proposition that the jubilee actually comes from the period of the monarchy. Although Bess believes that the

1.   W. Robertson Smith, in H.M. Orlinsky (ed.), *Lectures on the Religion of the Semites* (The Library of Biblical Studies; New York: Ktav, 3rd edn, 1969), pp. 77-101.

2.   G. von Rad, *Old Testament Theology* (trans. D.M.G. Stalker; 2 vols.; New York: Harper & Row, 1962–65), I, p. 299.

3.   Alt, 'Origins of Israelite Law', pp. 164-65.

4.   N.P. Lemche, 'The Manumission of Slaves—The Fallow Year—The Sabbatical Year—The Jobel Year', *VT* 26 (1976), p. 50.

5.   See Alt, 'Origins of Israelite Law', pp. 166-67; von Waldow, 'Social Responsibility', p. 195.

6.   Alt, 'Origins of Israelite Law', p. 166 n. 119.

jubilee's origins are in the premonarchic period, he concedes that a strong case can be made that it was developed early in the monarchy, when the king had the power to make such a decree which was necessary in an increasingly complex and stratified economy.[1] Indeed Gnuse contends that one cannot project the jubilee back to the era of settlement because it presupposes certain economic conditions (for example, private property and social stratification) which did not exist until the monarchy.[2] However, Gnuse's argument assumes that during the settlement period Israel was unaffected by the economic structures of its neighbors, some of whom lived within the boundaries of Israelite occupation. As soon as an entity which could be called Israel came into existence, it would have experienced pressures from the commercialized economies of its neighbors to adopt systems more compatible to them. Something very much like the jubilee could have arisen almost immediately in order to counteract those pressures. Also, a king was not necessary to create such regulations. Therefore, there is no reason to confine the origins of the jubilee to the monarchical period, and there is sufficient evidence to suggest that the world-view held by the premonarchic Israelites contained the necessary ingredients for creating the jubilee.

By the time Israel came into existence, many of these concepts had already undergone much change, but it seems that Israel held tenaciously to the notion that family land was inalienable and could not become a simple commodity to be bought or sold at will—a belief that is exemplified by the story of Naboth's vineyard (1 Kgs 21.1-19). That such traditions about land tenure were not only preserved but incorporated into important legal codes implies that these traditions were still able to explain the world adequately and provide a basis for an ethics of land ownership.

A traditio-historical analysis of the jubilee legislation as we find it in Leviticus 25 reveals a complex development.[3] The beginnings of the written law lie in the casuistic regulations dealing with the sale of landed property or of persons because of debt. Such persons or property were to experience a 'release' (*yôbēl*), but this release is not explained. As it now appears in Leviticus, this 'debt-sale law' lacks

1. Bess, 'Land Tenure', p. 143.
2. Gnuse, 'Jubilee Legislation in Leviticus', p. 46.
3. For a detailed analysis, see Fager, 'Land Tenure and the Biblical Jubilee', pp. 92-102.

any religious warrant and could very well have grown out of the community law of the 'village gate'. In the early exilic period, a redactor added details to 'the jubilee' (*hayyôbēl*) along with some theological warrant ('you shall fear your God'). Later in the exile, priestly editors adopted the jubilee laws for their own large legal corpus. These editors placed the jubilee in the context of the Sinai covenant and expressed the theological warrants (which were now expanded) in the second person plural. (For a detailed breakdown of Leviticus 25 into its constituent strata, see the Appendix.)

As the traditions developed, they accrued more and more theological warrants. Partly this must be viewed as compensation for the destabilization of the Israelite world; as the Israelites had greater difficulty in explaining their world, they tended to support the symbols that remained with divine sanctions. At the same time, provisions added to the law made it less practical to observe literally. We might be tempted to assume that this meant the legislation was being spiritualized and distanced from the 'real world'. A more adequate explanation of this evolution is that the course of Israelite history forced the compilers of the tradition to rely on the jubilee as an explanation of the real world which was hidden within the chaos of socio-political events. Thus, the jubilee became 'symbolic'—not in the sense of unreal but in the sense of truly real. I will examine how that happened during the exile in the following chapter.

Excursus

WAS IT EVER OBSERVED?

The jubilee is partly so intriguing because of what happened to it after reaching its final redaction in Leviticus 25, that is, how later generations responded to it. One biblical text that was written after Leviticus 25, and that one might expect to allude to the jubilee, is Neh. 5.1-13. In this text, Nehemiah is confronted by a situation of great economic disparity among the people, and the solution he proposes is an isolated reform, not necessarily to be repeated (Neh. 5.9-11). However, this text does not allude to any sabbath or jubilee laws, and the fact that this situation arises implies that neither the sabbath year nor the jubilee year had been observed for some time. The connections that do exist between Neh. 5.1-13 and Leviticus 25 concern the debt-sale laws, which, in their original form, have more to do with individual transactions than a general and recurrent economic reform.[1] The reform of Nehemiah 5 is so different

---

1.   Lemche, 'Manumission of Slaves', pp. 53-54.

from Leviticus 25 that they must not have emerged from the same economic milieu.[1] It is clear that, at this point in Israel's history, the jubilee had not been effective and that the political leadership made no use of it in appropriate situations. Thus, in the biblical literature, there is no evidence of the jubilee's emergence as a viable institution.

In the intertestamental period, there are allusions to a general fallow year in Maccabees (1 Macc. 6.49, 53); however, no mention is made of any economic reforms that were associated with the jubilee. The book of *Jubilees* (written sometime between 135 and 105 BCE) is based on the cycle of jubilee years, but little more is made of the jubilee than a measuring device for history which is carefully divided into 'jubilee' units which are further subdivided into 'sabbath' units. North suggests that the book of *Jubilees* took the social reform of Leviticus 25 as a unique event that was commemorated by subsequent jubilees through festival observance.[2] However, given the scope of the content of the book, it cannot be determined with certainty what the author's attitude toward the jubilee was. Coming from an eschatologically oriented community (Qumran), the author may have had little interest in recurrent social reforms like the jubilee. But for whatever reasons, the only use for the jubilee found in the intertestamental literature was as a chronological measuring device.

Ancient commentators living near the turn of the era add little more to the history of the jubilee. Philo made the connection between humanitarian deeds and the number seven (a particularly holy number), but it is not known if this originated in the biblical text or came from Greek philosophy.[3] In both his *Antiquities* and the *Jewish Wars*, Josephus makes several references to the observance of a general fallow year, but they are so vague and sometimes contradictory that little historical value can be attributed to them.[4] Regarding the jubilee itself, he makes only general comments not directly claiming any compliance. He does explain that the name 'jubilee' denoted 'liberty', and that at the jubilee a calculation of the balance between expenses and income of the land was made. If the balance was even or there was a profit, the land simply reverted to the original owner, but if there was a loss, the original owner paid the balance to the one to whom he had sold it before recovering the land.[5] But did that ever actually occur? At one point, Josephus states, 'There is still no one of the

---

1.   North, *Sociology of the Biblical Jubilee*, p. 206.

2.   North, *Sociology of the Biblical Jubilee*, pp. 71-73.

3.   North, *Sociology of the Biblical Jubilee*, pp. 76-78.

4.   In describing Antiochus's campaign against Bethsura and Jerusalem in the *Antiquities* (12.9.5), he mentions a lack of provisions due to a fallow year, but no such reference is made in his description in the *Jewish Wars* (1.1.5). He also refers to special hardships caused by the fallow year in descriptions of Hyrcanus's siege of the fortress Dagon (*Ant.* 13.8.1; *War* 1.2.4) Herod's siege of Jerusalem (*Ant.* 14.16.2; 15.1.2). Josephus also claims that both Alexander the Great and Julius Caesar granted the Jews a remission of their tribute on the seventh year because of the fallow law (*Ant.* 11.8.6; and 14.10.6). See R. North, 'Maccabean Sabbath Years', *Bib* 34 (1953), pp. 511-14, for the conclusion that Josephus is rather useless as true historical evidence.

5.   Josephus, *Ant.* 3.12.3.

Hebrews, who does not act even now as if Moses were present and ready to punish him if he should do any thing that is indecent'.[1] Such a rhetorically laden statement can hardly be taken as evidence that the jubilee was literally observed.

The two religious traditions that considered the Hebrew Bible a sacred text took rather different views of the jubilee. Several of the church fathers treated the jubilee allegorically—for example, often understanding the release of the fiftieth year as the general resurrection. On the other hand, others took the jubilee to be exclusively messianic, 'prophetic legislation' prefiguring the era of redemption and not to be taken materialistically.[2] In neither view was the jubilee seen as a social institution that was to affect the economic life of the community; rather it was highly abstracted in order to make it a religious symbol expressing Christian doctrine. The Talmud took a much more historical approach. The Talmud assumes that the sabbath years and the jubilee years were carefully counted from the occupation to the exile (*'Arak.* 12b). However, following the exile, because the Jews were not all settled in their proper tribal territories, the laws of the jubilee did not apply, but the jubilees were counted 'to keep the years of release holy' (*'Arak.* 32b). In the case of the Jewish scholars, the jubilee was literal legislation intended to affect the economic life of the community, but only when that community was demographically situated in the manner prescribed by the law in the first place. The jubilee year carried its own sanctity which had to be maintained, but it was no longer an institution for social reform.

---

1.   Josephus, *Ant.* 3.15.3.
2.   North, *Sociology of the Biblical Jubilee*, pp. 225-29.

Part II

A SOCIOLOGICAL ANALYSIS OF THE JUBILEE IN THE LATE EXILIC
PERIOD

Chapter 3

THE EXILE

The synchronic analysis will take a 'slice' out of the growth of the jubilee tradition and examine one particular period in that growth. For this case study, that slice will come from the exilic period when the priests redacted the already existing jubilee laws and formed Leviticus 25 in much the way we have it today.[1] This study will examine the priests themselves, looking at who they were and what function they performed in their society. By examining how the priests fit into the social dynamics of the exilic community, we can form hypotheses regarding their own motivations and interests—motivations and interests that are part of the factors that determined the way in which the priests handled the jubilee. Such hypotheses must be carefully constructed on the basis of what social science already knows about groups like the priests within societies like ancient Israel during periods like the exile. (That is to say that any claims about psychological states of ancient people have to be tentative.)

To aid in pinpointing the priests' position, it is helpful to compare their expression of land tenure traditions with that of a contemporary group, namely Ezekiel and his disciples. In Ezek. 47.12–48.29, an 'Ezekielian school' described the establishment of a land system that would form the base of a stable community once the people had returned from exile. It is to our advantage that the Ezekielian school is related to, yet distinguishable from, the priestly school so that there are both points of comparison and points of contrast. Because of the similarities between Ezekiel and P, the differences highlight the

1.   A tradio-historical analysis of Leviticus 25 would show that, except for a few minor additions (which made no substantive changes), the jubilee land laws as we now have them were formed during the late exilic period by the 'priestly writers'. (See Fager, 'Land Tenure and the Biblical Jubilee', pp. 84-106.)

distinctiveness of the priestly views and provide a clearer view of their own world-view.

There can be little doubt that the Babylonian exile of Israel was an extremely important period in the history of the people and the development of their self-understanding. Certainly, it represents only one phase in a longer history of the dispersion of Jews, which began with the fall of Samaria in 722 BCE and actually accelerated during the Persian and Hellenistic periods.[1] However, the Babylonian exile is quite significant in that it began the era of 'Jewish colonialism', which refers both to the colonization of Jews outside Palestine and to the colonial rule imposed upon Palestine by foreign empires.[2] As the details of the nature of the exile are discussed below, it will become clear that this event required a fresh, clear articulation of the Yahwistic tradition in order to keep it alive.

Sixth-Century Ferment

The sixth century was an era of great creativity throughout much of the world, and the people of Israel participated in that movement. The trading activities of the sixth century led to the expansion of a merchant class which was not dependent on the state, the possession of land or the status of birth for its base of economic power. The existence of such an independent class led, in turn, to greater independence of thought.[3] Amid the wide variety of thought expressed in the intellectual activity of the sixth century, there existed a common theme—'the search for a single principle to explain all phenomena'.[4] Perhaps as a reaction against the independent thinkers or perhaps as a part of the search for a unifying principle, there was a powerful archaizing tendency among the Babylonian kings (culminating in Nabonidus) and among the kings of the Twenty-Sixth Dynasty in

---

1. N.K. Gottwald, *The Hebrew Bible: A Socio-Literary Introduction* (Philadelphia: Fortress Press, 1985), p. 201.

2. Gottwald, *The Hebrew Bible*, p. 421.

3. J.M. Davison, 'The Oikoumene in Ferment: A Cross-Cultural Study of the Sixth Century', in C. Evans, W. Hallo and J. White (eds.), *Scripture in Context: Essays on the Comparative Method* (Pittsburgh Theological Monograph Series, 34; Pittsburgh: Pickwick Press, 1980), p. 209.

4. Davison, 'The Oikoumene in Ferment', p. 201.

Egypt.[1] Israel was not immune to these same forces; a similar kind of independence would have been experienced by the Jews as their social structure was torn apart—the ruling class taken into exile and the normal forms of social and political power stripped from them. We will see below how the priestly writers echo this tendency.

However, it is only an echo. Taking note of Israel's lack of any monumental or documentary history, Jean Davison argues that, unlike the fossilizing antiquarian movements of Egypt and Babylonia, 'Israel's quest for its purer beginnings resulted in the creation of a spiritual past which ensured itself a future even without the recovery of political independence'.[2] It is too much to say that Israel lacked *any* monumental or documentary history; for example, the temple was a monument to the people of Israel, and there was a strong movement to rebuild it. But it can be said that Israel had not invested its national identity in monumental or documentary history nearly to the extent of the major empires. Indeed, the very fact of being in exile proved that political possession of the land was unnecessary for being the people of God, and that realization helped form an understanding of Yahwism that transcended the parochialism that dominated the ancient Near Eastern religions (particularly in the smaller states).[3] Thus Israel was a part of a general ferment during the sixth century, and it contributed its own features which brought Yahwism to new life.

The Historical Picture

It is widely recognized that the exiles consisted of the upper and ruling classes and that those left behind to rebuild the devastated land were the peasants. Morton Smith argues that within these exiled classes were found most of the leaders of the 'Yahweh-alone' party;[4] therefore, the very persons who were able and willing to perform the task of preserving and transmitting the Yahwistic traditions were in Babylonia. Of course, some literature from the Yahwistic tradition was produced in Palestine (Jeremiah was among those left behind), and many of the exiles were ready to abandon their tradition (note

1. Davison, 'The Oikoumene in Ferment', p. 202.
2. Davison, 'The Oikoumene in Ferment', p. 210.
3. J. Landousies, 'Le don de la terre de Palestine', *NRT* 99 (1976), pp. 326-28.
4. M. Smith, *Palestinian Parties and Politics that Shaped the Old Testament* (New York: Columbia University Press, 1971), p. 99.

Deutero-Isaiah's polemic against the apostates). Nevertheless, much of the intellectual power that produced the Israelite literature of the sixth century experienced the exile away from the homeland and under the direct control of the Babylonian rulers.

There is little direct evidence of the conditions under which the exiles lived. However, the indirect evidence from Ezekiel and Jeremiah suggests that during the early years the exiles enjoyed a reasonable degree of freedom; settling in their own communities and amassing some wealth.[1] Within those communities, they were able to manage their own affairs with little Babylonian interference.[2] On the one hand, this situation allowed the Jewish community to preserve their traditions free from pressures to conform to the Babylonian culture. Therefore, those intellectuals who were wont to do so (I shall examine them more closely below) were free both to gather any documents they were able to bring with them and to transcribe the oral traditions they remembered. On the other hand, a situation of *relative* freedom can be a powerful lure toward the empire 'graciously' granting that freedom as well as concealing the genuine threat to one's own cultural identity. Ezekiel was quite active during the early years of the exile but otherwise it is difficult to date much material to that period. It appears that much of the creativity of the exile came after Nebuchadrezzar's death when conditions became less stable.

The 'relativity' of their freedom must not be overstated; Israel was a society in crisis. Societies deal with problems constantly, but as long as those problems are considered solved, there is no motivation to alter their solutions.[3] However, in order to maintain the common knowledge used in the solutions of a society's problems, the social structure must be preserved.[4] As stated earlier, every society requires a social foundation upon which social knowledge rests, and if that foundation becomes weaker, the need for bolstering society's

1. P. Ackroyd, *Exile and Restoration* (OTL; Philadelphia: Westminster Press, 1968), pp. 31-32.

2. B. Oded, 'Judah and the Exile', in J. Hayes and J.M. Miller (eds.), *Israelite and Judean History* (OTL; Philadelphia: Westminster Press, 1977), p. 483.

3. A. Schutz and T. Luckmann, *The Structures of the Life-World* (trans. R.M. Zaner and H.T. Englhardt, Jr; Evanston: Northwestern University Press, 1973), p. 296.

4. Schutz and Luckmann, *The Structures of the Life-World*, p. 297.

knowledge about the world becomes greater.[1] Israel's social base was in a shambles. As the Jews formed a community in Babylon, they also formed a social structure; however, the basic legitimating institution, the monarchy, had been destroyed.

The exile created serious theological problems for Israel because of the events accompanying it—the destruction of the temple, the end of the Davidic dynasty, the loss of the land, the apparent invalidation of the Sinai covenant, the decimation of the priesthood and the end of sacrifice.[2] These events called into question the generally accepted proposition that life is orderly and that people can live effectively within a comprehensible world.[3] The exiles, who found themselves transported into a very different culture, were exposed to a society that actually thought differently, graphically pointing out to them that their own concept of the world was not inevitable.[4] If their concept of the world was not inevitable, the Jews must have asked themselves whether any world-view was absolute or whether the world had no order.[5] The radical 'de-legitimation' of their social structure threatened the Jews with the meaninglessness of a chaotic universe.

To compound their problems, even their relative freedom seems to have deteriorated in the latter part of the exile. The risk of an inherited monarchy is that the successor will not possess the qualities of leadership that made the predecessor great. Although Amel-Marduk had been 'groomed' to succeed Nebuchadrezzar, he did not have the aggressive leadership that allowed his father and grandfather to build the Babylonian empire. Amel-Marduk's reign was short and ineffective, a situation which caused consternation among Jews seeking security in Babylon and anticipation among Jews seeking to return to Judah.[6] However, a powerful member of the court, Nergal-shar-usur, murdered Amel-Marduk and usurped the throne, saving Babylonia from disintegration. In fact, during the four years of Nergal-shar-usur's reign,

1.   Berger, *The Sacred Canopy*, p. 47.
2.   R.W. Klein, *Israel in Exile: A Theological Interpretation*, (Overtures to Biblical Theology; Philadelphia: Fortress Press, 1979), pp. 3-5.
3.   See Geertz, *The Interpretation of Culture*, p. 100.
4.   See Mannheim, *Ideology and Utopia*, p. 7; and Berger and Luckmann, *The Social Construction of Reality*, p. 100.
5.   See Berger, *The Sacred Canopy*, pp. 22-24, 31; and Harrod, *The Human Center*, p. 96.
6.   J.D. Newsome, *By the Waters of Babylon: An Introduction to the History and Theology of the Exile* (Atlanta: John Knox, 1979), pp. 92-97.

he was able to restore the empire to the power it had enjoyed under Nebuchadrezzar.[1] This temporarily allayed the fears of some of the Jews and stifled the hopes of others. However, it must be emphasized that this renewed strength was only temporary. Peter Ackroyd is correct in concluding that, after Nebuchadrezzar's death in 562, the quality of leadership declined leading to the succession of four kings in six years, the last being Nabonidus who was placed on the throne in 556.[2]

Nabonidus, who came from Haran and whose mother was a priestess of the moon god Sin, usurped the Babylonian throne one year after Nergal-shar-usur's death, but alienated the political leadership by his long absence from Babylon and the religious leadership by his apparent neglect of Marduk and his cult.[3] Of course, the literature about Nabonidus comes from his enemies; we must not therefore rely too heavily on the harsh criticism of him found on the cylinders from the Persian period. The precise effects of his policies on the strength of the empire are difficult to determine; however, subjective responses are sometimes more important to the progress of history than objective facts. Therefore, what Nabonidus's subjects perceived his policies to be would have been crucial to their support (or lack of support) of him. This is equally true for the non-Babylonians living under his rule.

For the religious life of the community in exile, the most important of Nabonidus's policies was his attitude toward religious plurality. Bustenay Oded argues that 'there is no clear and explicit evidence' that the exiles were ever subjected to political or religious suppression during their time in Babylon.[4] As we saw above, the Jews enjoyed relative autonomy during the time of Nebuchadrezzar's reign, and there are no clear references to religious persecution in the anti-Nabonidus literature of the Persians—he was merely accused of neglecting the cult of Marduk. One might assume that if there were grounds to condemn Nabonidus for religious persecution, his enemies certainly would have done so. However, that literature only deals with Babylonian and Persian concerns; the plight of subject peoples is not revealed in those cylinders. It is possible that Nabonidus, a devotee of Sin, did not feel at liberty actually to suppress the Marduk cult but did persecute the religious adherents of non-Babylonian sects.

1. Newsome, *By the Waters of Babylon*, pp. 99-100.
2. Ackroyd, *Exile and Restoration*, p. 19.
3. Newsome, *By the Waters of Babylon*, pp. 105-109.
4. Oded, 'Judah and the Exile', p. 483.

If we are looking for 'clear and explicit' evidence for such a persecution, then Oded is correct in declaring that none exists; however, there is enough indirect evidence to suggest the probability of a change in policy towards intolerance of religious plurality. Evidence exists that suggests Nabonidus was actually a strong king who had a definite political and religious program and was willing to use oppressive measures to achieve his goals.[1] A weak king may elicit a coup d'état but not the kind of polemics found on the Persian cylinders. There is some indirect evidence that Nabonidus attempted to achieve a greater religious uniformity throughout the empire which was unpopular among the Babylonians and oppressive to the exiles. First, the narratives found in the first half of Daniel may actually be recollections of repressive measures taken by Nabonidus and projected back onto Nebuchadrezzar.[2] Secondly, Deutero-Isaiah's polemic against idols may reflect the pressures felt by the Jewish community to conform to Nabonidus's religious program.[3] Thirdly, Deutero-Isaiah also makes many allusions to the harsh treatment being suffered by the exiles (40.2; 41.11-12; 42.7, 22; 47.6; 49.9, 13, 24-26; 51.7, 13-14, 23). Finally, Babylonia is singled out as the protypical 'evil empire'.[4] Certainly the destruction of Jerusalem and the exile itself would generate much ill will on the part of the Jews, but the fact that Babylonia takes Egypt's place as *the* enemy of Yahweh might indicate further oppression during this time.

What Nabonidus actually did is not clear, but it appears from the Israelite literature of the time that the Jews *felt* persecuted. Again, their perceptions are more influential on their response to the situation than the objective facts; therefore, if they perceived themselves to be oppressed, they would have responded accordingly. Under such conditions, the threat to the existence of the tradition becomes acute and efforts to record that tradition are redoubled. Periods of persecution are not the only times when traditions are reformulated, but it is during such periods that a concerted effort is made to ground the tradition on a solid footing or to save it from possible loss. I shall

1.   J.M. Wilkie, 'Nabonidus and the Later Jewish Exiles', *JTS* NS 2 (1951), pp. 39-41.
2.   Wilkie, 'Nabonidus and the Exiles', p. 142; P. Ackroyd, *Exile and Restoration*, p. 37.
3.   Wilkie, 'Nabonidus and the Exiles', pp. 41-42.
4.   Wilkie, 'Nabonidus and the Exiles', pp. 37-38.

examine how the priests attempted to do this below.

Into this milieu was interjected a historical datum which must have had a tremendous impact on the exiles' attitudes—the rise of Cyrus. Cyrus was immediately recognized on the international scene as a budding young conqueror with whom all the world would have to contend. Shortly after Cyrus overthrew his grandfather, Astyages, Croesus formed an alliance with Egypt, Babylonia and Sparta to stop Cyrus's move to the west.[1] The Jewish exiles would have known that there was someone on the move in the world who had the potential of breaking their bonds. Cyrus may not have turned out to be the enlightened liberator as he is often portrayed,[2] but for the exiles Cyrus's actual policy was less important than the fact that he could end Nabonidus's rule. As under the rule of Amel-Marduk, there was a diversity of attitudes within the Jewish community. For those who had tied their own welfare to that of Babylonia, there was either fear that the Babylonian status quo would be disrupted, or hope that Cyrus would reinvigorate the Babylonian economy, but for those who were dissatisfied with life in exile, there was the hope that the fall of Babylon would result in a return to Judah.[3] Thus, in what turned out to be the closing years of the exile, the Jews were struggling to maintain their religious identity, motivated by a threat to the survival of Yahwism and a hope that they would soon be able to worship Yahweh freely.

Response

How did the people respond to this threat to their orderly world? Although the focus of our attention will be on the exiles in Babylonia, some of the responses by those left in Palestine would have affected the literature being produced in Babylon. It is probable that not all the landed citizens and officials were taken into exile, but the proportion which was taken was large enough to effect major social changes in the homeland. Those who are often labelled as the 'poor of the land' would have enjoyed more political influence under Babylonian authority than under Davidic rule, and formerly propertyless peasants

---

1. Newsome, *By the Waters of Babylon*, pp. 111-12.
2. A. Kuhrt, 'The Cyrus Cylinder and Achaemenid Imperial Policy', *JSOT* 25 (1983), pp. 83-97.
3. Newsome, *By the Waters of Babylon*, pp. 113-14.

became landholders.[1] Gottwald believes that, with most of the officials in exile, the premonarchic village tribalism (which had been suppressed by the monarchy) 'was able to re-emerge as the dominant force in organizing and preserving Palestinian Jewish identity throughout the exile'.[2] If Gottwald means a return to his hypothetical egalitarian society of the twelfth and eleventh centuries, that can hardly be the case; too many centuries had elapsed and the Babylonians would not have allowed it. However, it would be correct to say that village norms took greater prominence (vis-à-vis urban norms) in the formation of a new social structure in Palestine. That would have meant greater equality among the people both economically and politically, but care must be taken not to overstate the case.

Not only was the legitimacy of the ruling classes brought into question by the fall of Judah, but the legitimacy of Yahwism was also threatened. In response to the disaster, many returned to older, indigenous cults; one may note Jeremiah's polemic against the Queen of Heaven in ch. 44 and the Deuteronomic and Holiness materials' stress on the destruction of Canaan.[3] Even among those who retained a belief in Yahweh at all, many turned to a syncretistic religion which included Canaanite and/or Babylonian elements.[4] It may have been that the 'people of the land' were already participating in syncretistic cults,[5] and with the destruction of the central government, there were no more restraints on this practice. However, as Jeremiah 44 indicates, the downturn in Judah's fortunes at the beginning of the sixth century caused many to lose confidence in an exclusively Yahwistic cult. The power of Yahweh to hold their world together had been compromised.

Yet Yahwism did not die in Palestine. The condition of the temple and the temple cult is not at all clear for the exilic period, but it seems evident that some sort of religious activity occurred at the site.[6] According to ancient thought the site itself was sacred regardless of the presence of a building; therefore, sacrifice would have still been

---

1.   Ackroyd, *Exile and Restoration*, pp. 23-24.
2.   Gottwald, *The Hebrew Bible*, p. 425.
3.   Ackroyd, *Exile and Restoration*, pp. 40-41.
4.   G. Fohrer, *History of Israelite Religion* (trans. D.E. Green; Nashville: Abingdon Press, 1972), pp. 309-10.
5.   See Smith, *Palestinian Parties and Politics*.
6.   Ackroyd, *Exile and Restoration*, pp. 25-29.

appropriate at the sacred site and was probably still offered.[1] Jeremiah refers to men coming from Shechem, Shiloh and Samaria to present cereal offerings and incense to the temple (41.4-5); therefore, there were those who remained faithful to the Yahwistic tradition. However, a sacred site needs sacred priests. Nigel Allan presents a convincing case that while the ruling priests of the Jerusalem cult (the Zadokites) were in exile, Levitical priests from the Judean countryside took over the priestly function at the holy site, to the dismay of the exiled Zadokites.[2] There was a Yahwism in Palestine to which the intelligentsia in exile could relate, but it was a Yahwism that was beginning to depart from the official structures approved by the elite.

Of course, the religious officials in exile also had to be concerned about the response of their fellow exiles. The exiles not only faced the same threat to Yahwism's legitimacy as those left in Palestine, they also carried the burden of geographical separation from the sacred site, where mere proximity could reinforce one's faith. James Newsome lists three typical forms of response among the exiles; (1) capitulation to Babylonian theology (cf. Isa. 44.9-20 and Ezek. 20.32); (2) despairing resignation; or (3) a mixture of hope and despair, that is, an inability to abandon the old traditions yet an inability to 'derive meaning or succor from them'.[3] For many of the exiles the victory of Babylonia meant the defeat of Yahwism, and they adopted the Babylonian order rather than be left with the chaos left in the wake of Jerusalem's destruction.

One of the hardships faced by the exiles (particularly the first group of deportees) was their growing alienation from those living in the homeland, people who seemed to cut them off from their roots and their identity (cf. Ezek. 15.1-8 and Jeremiah 24).[4] During the decade following the first deportation, it was often believed that those exiles were the ones being punished for Judah's sins. This became more difficult to believe after the destruction of Jerusalem, yet those who remained in Palestine still made the claim that the exiles had been

---

1. Fohrer, *History of Israelite Religion*, p. 310.
2. N. Allan, 'The Identity of the Jerusalem Priesthood during the Exile', *HeyJ* 23 (1982), pp. 259-69.
3. Newsome, *By the Waters of Babylon*, p. 72. Cf. Ackroyd, *Exile and Restoration*, pp. 41-42.
4. Newsome, *By the Waters of Babylon*, pp. 75-76.

expelled from the cultic community (cf. Ezek. 11.14-17).[1] Not only did this add to the exiles' sense of alienation from the ritual that made them a part of the Yahwistic community, it also seems that 'participation in the cult was somehow connected with the legal right to the land'.[2] This increased the threat to the exiles' belief in an orderly world and led either to greater despair or to a backlash which will be explored below.

One form of backlash was the development of rituals that could be practiced away from the sacred place in Judah. In the absence of the temple and its sacrifice, there arose a substitute institution—later to become the synagogue—in which the people congregated for a simple type of worship which included prayer, hymns and a lecture.[3] The exiles literally created a Yahwistic community in Babylonia which had its own integrity apart from the religious structure that existed in Palestine. In this new congregation, they were able to re-establish their ties to the tradition and reinforce the world as they understood it. In addition to forming such an institution, the exiles focused their attentions on rituals that could be practiced away from the temple site proper. Observance of the Sabbath, circumcision and purity laws all helped distinguish the Jews from the foreign people among whom they lived and aided them in maintaining their identity as Yahweh's people.[4] In a world that seemed to be tottering on the brink of chaos, such rituals kept the exiles linked to the faith of their ancestors by connecting them to the very mind of God.[5] This bond was necessary in order to maintain the meaningfulness of the Yahwistic world otherwise shattered by the Babylonian conquest.

Besides responding to the exilic situation through these institutional and ritualistic means, some also responded literarily. The two most comprehensive attempts to reorder the world were the Deuteronomistic and the priestly writings. These two works did not spring into being *ex nihilo* during the exile, but they grew out of materials that were treasured by particular segments of the Israelite society, each with its

1.   J. Blenkinsopp, *A History of Prophecy in Israel* (Philadelphia: Westminster Press, 1983), p. 180.

2.   Smith, *Palestinian Parties and Politics*, p. 100. See also Blenkinsopp, *A History of Prophecy*, p. 180.

3.   Fohrer, *History of Israelite Religion*, p. 113.

4.   Fohrer, *History of Israelite Religion*, p. 312.

5.   Newsome, *By the Waters of Babylon*, pp. 101-104.

own understanding of how the world worked.[1] Of concern to this study is the priestly response which will be discussed in detail below.

In conclusion, all these responses were attempts to restabilize the world. Much of the Israelite ideology rested upon the inviolability of Jerusalem and the Davidic dynasty. With the fall of both, the world suddenly became a mysterious place where one could not count on the accepted rules of order to hold.[2] During the exile, external pressures and internal strife reached a crisis point, forcing the defenders of Yahwism to 'construct a secure, unassailable position from which all doubts about God's government of the world could be repulsed and refuted'.[3] In addition, when one inhabits a society which lacks a religious monopoly, then one must construct a sub-society to function as the social foundation that undergirds one's religious order, otherwise conversion becomes more likely.[4] Lacking the core rituals of the temple cult, the exiles turned to ideological and philosophical foundations to reinterpret the meaning of their history and to legitimate Yahwism in the new world.[5]

It appears that this attempt to relegitimate the Yahwistic world was, at least in part, successful; expressions of hope began to be articulated

1.   O.H. Steck (Theological Streams of Tradition', in D.A. Knight [ed.], *Tradition and Theology in the Old Testament* [Philadelphia: Fortress Press, 1977], pp. 206-207) provides an outline of the 'streams of tradition' as they moved through Israel's history. Steck claims that the streams expressed among the exiles (prophetic activation of priestly concepts and the priestly history) looked toward an orderly cosmos in which salvation would soon be restored, which must be contrasted with the Deuteronomistic notion (which he locates in Judah) of sin, guilt, and the necessity for repentance. For excellent discussions of the responses these two groups made to the exile, see Ackroyd, *Exile and Restoration*, pp. 62-102, and Klein, *Israel in Exile,* pp. 23-43, 125-48.

2.   See P. Ackroyd, 'Continuity and Discontinuity: Rehabilitation and Authentication', in D. Knight (ed.), *Tradition and Theology in the Old Testament,* pp. 215-34, for an excellent discussion of what happens when one's world loses its stability.

3.   W. Eichrodt, 'Faith in Providence and Theodicy in the Old Testament', in J. Crenshaw (ed.), *Theodicy in the Old Testament* (Philadelphia: Fortress Press, 1983), p. 32.

4.   Berger, *The Sacred Canopy*, pp. 49-50.

5.   Newsome, *By the Waters of Babylon*, pp. 97-98; D.W. Thomas, 'The Sixth Century BC: A Creative Epoch in the History of Israel', *JSS* 6 (1961), pp. 33-46; Harrod, *The Human Center*, pp. 103-4; Berger and Luckmann, *The Social Construction of Reality,* p. 99.

more and more as responses to the exile. One concrete example is found in an inscription from that period which reads, 'belonging to Yehoyishma daughter of Sawas-sar-usuz'. The father's name is Babylonian, but the daughter's name (which means 'Yahweh will hear') expresses belief in Yahweh and the hope that Yahweh will redeem the people.[1] The prophets of the exile maintained the people's religious identity by proclaiming that the catastrophe had occurred, not because the Babylonian gods had defeated Yahweh, but because the one God of the universe had punished them for their sin but now would restore them in a new age of security and peace.[2] Walther Zimmerli also claims that 'the institution of a divinely decreed year of release' became the foundation of great hope for the exiles.[3] Undoubtedly, the rise of Cyrus elicited much of the hope we find expressed in the exilic literature (see the comments on Cyrus above), but without a comprehensible Yahwistic world for which to hope, the exiles could not have maintained their religious identity, and they would have become just part of the Babylonian crowd welcoming the conquering hero.

Looking toward Restoration

As hope became a part of the exiles' response to their situation, some reflection on their future—in particular how restoration could be effected—took on greater importance. Gottwald lists three factors that were to complicate the returnees' task of rebuilding the nation,[4] two of which could very well have been foreseen by the exiles. First, the Persians were dealing with a huge empire that comprised many different ethnic groups, cultures and religions. The Persians' need to maintain a unified empire while allowing these groups a degree of cultural autonomy would have forced those peoples to walk a narrow path between their own nationalistic inclinations and capitulation to Persian domination. The Israelites had had previous experience in walking such

---

1.   Oded, 'Judah and the Exile', p. 486.
2.   Oded, 'Judah and the Exile', pp. 484-85; Fohrer, *History of Israelite Religion*, pp. 327-29.
3.   W. Zimmerli, 'Das "Gnadenjahr des Herrn" ', in A. Kuschke and E . Kutsch (eds.), *Archäologie und Altes Testament: Festschrift für Kurt Galling* (Tübingen: Mohr, 1970), p. 328.
4.   Gottwald, *The Hebrew Bible*, p. 429.

a path, but there is no evidence that they considered this issue before they actually returned to Judah. Secondly, the socio-economic fabric of Judah had been severely damaged by the Babylonian conquest and the exile of the leadership. It is clear from the books of Ezra and Nehemiah that this issue was well understood as the restoration was beginning. Given the communication between Babylon and Palestine, it seems unlikely that the economic conditions could have been ignored, and that appears to be part of the reason for the jubilee legislation. Finally, the tension between the Palestinian Jews and the returnees created a delicate political situation. As noted above, the exiles felt alienated from the Palestinians, who believed the exiles had been expelled from the community. The main issue involved here was whether reconciliation could take place or whether one group would dominate the other.

The competition among groups extends beyond that between the Palestinians and the returnees. The variety of material which has come from this era is evidence that there were several distinct groups among the returnees whom Smith calls the 'Yahweh-alone party'.[1] Discussion concerning the identity and nature of such groups is not at an end,[2] and clear boundaries among them are still impossible to draw. However, even though these groups may have been very loosely associated, certain people had particular agenda for the future. As these groups recognized the real possibility for a return to the homeland, they would have begun to formulate their philosophies and ideologies that undergirded their respective beliefs about how the restoration ought to take place. This study will examine one of those groups and one subgroup within it.

1. Smith, *Palestinian Parties and Politics*, pp. 101-102.
2. Smith, *Palestinian Parties and Politics*; P.D. Hanson, *The Diversity of Scripture: A Theological Interpretation* (Overtures to Biblical Theology; Philadelphia: Fortress Press, 1982), pp. 14-62; and O. Plöger, *Theology and Eschatology* (trans. S. Rudman; Richmond, VA: John Knox, 1968).

Chapter 4

THE PRIESTS AND THEIR LITERATURE

Assuming that the priestly work was produced late in the exilic period
in Babylonia, it is important to comment on the social function of the
group we call 'the priests'. The purpose of P is basically threefold:
(1) to preserve the ancient traditions now endangered by the
Babylonian conquest, (2) to explain that conquest in terms of divine
punishment, and (3) to provide a foundation for proper living in the
future (as is especially seen in P's use of the Holiness Code).[1] The
jubilee land laws were used by P to perform this threefold function in
the social milieu of the exile for the sake of the community and in
order to promote some of their own interests.

The Intelligentsia

As Mannheim points out, every society has one or more groups who
must interpret the world for the society, and this group may be called
the 'intelligentsia'.[2] For centuries before the exile, the priests had an
important teaching function, and it is clear from the priestly work that
the priests understood themselves to be interpreters of the world.
Other groups performed these functions, for example, the sages, but
the priests worked from a specifically cultic/legal context. Even in exile,
it appears that they did not do this individually but, as other cultic
professionals, congregated in particular settlements, for example,
Casiphia (Ezra 8.15-20).[3] Regardless of how structured the organization was, these priests certainly had been institutionalized in that they
performed socially recognized and accepted acts within the specific role
of 'priest' and they had a shared history that was an integral part of

1. Porter, *Leviticus*, pp. 7-8.
2. Mannheim, *Ideology and Utopia*, p. 10.
3. Oded, 'Judah and the Exile', p. 483.

the identity of the institution.[1] In addition, as experts in a narrow sector of knowledge, they created highly theoretical legitimations of their institution—legitimations which finally transcended pragmatic concerns so that the institution functioned in such and such a manner, not because it worked, but because it was right.[2] Of course, the specific functions and individual abilities of the many priests must have varied considerably, but this study is concerned with those priests who participated in the task of collecting, reinterpreting and reformulating the old traditions.

The priests' relationship with other forms of authority was ambiguous. There was no Israelite monarchy to support or deny the priestly interpretations of the world; therefore, within the Jewish community itself, there were no institutions with coercive power to proclaim the legitimacy of the priests—there were only informal (but well-established) groups, such as prophets, sages or 'elders'. While not all the exiles remained Yahwists, among those who did there were enough who recognized the priests' legitimacy to support the institution of the priesthood. On the other hand, the political authority of Babylonia appears to have turned against Yahwistic views when Nabonidus came to the throne and attempted to force religious uniformity on the empire. The priests constructed an alternative definition of reality to the Babylonian one and withdrew into a subsociety which acknowledged the priestly definition.[3] In a climate of competing world-views when the distribution of power is dependent on the outcome of the competition, knowledge becomes an important weapon in the struggle, placing the intelligentsia in the position of power brokers.[4]

The priests were not neutral observers in a power struggle in which they had no interests. The exiled priests had been a part of the power elite before the fall of Jerusalem, and when the hope arose that the Jews might be able to recreate a Jerusalem-based nation, the priests were active participants in the quest for control over that restoration. As the priests reinterpreted the world for the Jewish community, the priests' own interests must have affected their task; it is psychologically impossible for this not to have happened. The parts of a definition of

1. Berger and Luckmann, *The Social Construction of Reality*, pp. 51-52.
2. Berger and Luckmann, *The Social Construction of Reality*, pp. 107-109.
3. Berger and Luckmann, *The Social Construction of Reality*, pp. 115-17.
4. Schutz and Luckmann, *Structures of the Life-World*, p. 315.

reality that directly relate to the pragmatic concerns of a power interest will be modified for the sake of the interest.[1] If a particular definition of reality is related to a power interest, that definition is called an 'ideology'.[2] Thus, as the priests were reconstructing the Yahwistic world in anticipation of the restoration of the Jewish nation, they were also involved in the production of an ideology.

Geertz warns us not to take this notion of ideology too cynically; for the sake of adequate psychological equilibrium, people form 'symbolic outlets' which reorganize a disorganized world. An ideology structures those symbols in such a way as to conform to reality as it has been perceived.[3] The ideological salve that will soothe the wounds of psychological tension happens also to support the power interest of the group. Mannheim adds that the ideology held by a ruling class prevents them from recognizing any facts that would contradict their own definition of reality; any alternative definitions must be false.[4] The exiles had experienced a tremendous social disequilibrium, and they were engaged in an enormous struggle with Nabonidus for the power to determine their own identity. The priests were also in a power struggle over control of the restoration. The priests had to produce a world-view that could maintain the Yahwistic identity of the people (easing their psychological tension), and in the process they produced a world-view that maintained their place of power when the nation was to be restored. The priests would have considered any alternative views as defective. These two worlds are not necessarily incompatible, but it is necessary to recognize the distinction.

Bearers of the Tradition

Any symbolic universe (the Yahwistic world for the priests) orders history, creating a 'past' whose content and meaning the members of the community share.[5] As we have seen, it was one of the tasks of the priests to maintain and pass on that 'past', ensuring its proper transmission to the next generation. Such a transmission is interpretive by nature because it carries the meaning of an event from predecessors

---

1. Berger and Luckmann, *The Social Construction of Reality*, pp. 114-15.
2. Berger and Luckmann, *The Social Construction of Reality*, p. 113.
3. Geertz, *The Interpretation of Cultures*, pp. 202-13.
4. Mannheim, *Ideology and Utopia*, p. 40.
5. Berger and Luckmann, *The Social Construction of Reality*, p. 95.

who experienced it to successors who did not.[1] These successors who did not experience the historical event being transmitted by the tradition may recall the past as a thematic whole (in which old interpretations are taken for granted), or they may rehearse the past in its individual parts—reliving history.[2] The latter is most likely to occur during periods of social disturbance when the foundations of the community's world must be examined and reinterpreted. The priests, as bearers of the tradition, also reinterpreted it for a generation whose experience in history tended to discredit the world experienced by the predecessors. They had to recreate the Yahwistic tradition step by step in order to meet the demands of a radically different historical context.

Regarding the legal section of the Priestly Work (with which we are most concerned here), the laws were clearly linked to a covenant event at Mount Sinai. The priests did not invent Sinai as a place of religious importance; it was already firmly established in the tradition. However, the priests did re-emphasize it so that Sinai became the primary source for the legitimacy of the Yahwistic community. The priests located there laws and legal codes (for example, the jubilee laws of the Holiness Code) that had once been independent from the Sinai tradition. This hermeneutical act was a logical interpretation within the exilic context. Sinai was historically more remote than the establishment of the Davidic dynasty or the building of the temple; therefore, it was capable of taking on mythic proportions which were even less liable to delegitimation. Not only was the Sinai event semi-mythic historically, the mountain had become semi-mythic geographically. Certainly, it was a literal mountain, but its true location was now a mystery; therefore, Sinai could not be violated as Jerusalem and the temple had been, and the sacred source for the orderliness of the Jewish world was safe from pagan conquerors. Establishing the origin of the Jewish people during the wilderness period also allowed the exiles to identify with their predecessors more easily. As their ancestors did before them, the exiles were looking toward the creation of a community based on a Yahwistic world.

John Levenson contends that linking the law to Sinai added the flexibility needed to respond to the new situations faced by the exiles:

---

1.   See Harrod, *The Human Center*, p. 87.
2.   See Harrod, *The Human Center*, p. 24.

[Sinai] served as a source of continuity which enabled new norms to be promulgated with the authority of the old and enabled social change to take place without rupturing the sense of tradition and the continuity of historic identity.[1]

Since the Sinai event was already an accepted part of the tradition, the priests' reinterpreting it as *the* source of legitimacy for the law and the community did not sever the ties between the successors and their predecessors. The new generation could clearly maintain their identity as Yahwists, like their ancestors from ages past. The Yahwistic world had not been destroyed by the Babylonians; therefore, the disruption of the exile did not imply chaos. However, the priests were able to link new understandings of the law (understandings needed in the new context) to the ancient seat of legitimacy, making the legal system adaptable while appearing quite stable.

Of course, much of the priestly material is concerned with cultic matters. George Mendenhall believes that ritual functions dominated the priests' concept of the past and that they had little actual historical insight.[2] It is true that P's Sinai tradition is focused on the tabernacle, a proper priesthood and an effective system of rituals.[3] On the other hand, even though the rituals can become a means for a particular group to maintain prestige or power by controlling esoteric knowledge, ritual exists because it articulates basic beliefs about the cosmos. For the priests, the sacrificial rites were Yahweh's gift to the chosen people that expressed the bond between God and the nation.[4] Through its cultic life, the community continually reminded itself of the fundamental structure of the universe and grounded its moral understandings in that structure. Thus, even though the priests focused on ritual, the ritual was the bearer of a total world-view, including the community's morality.

At this point, we begin to see more clearly the effect of the priests' function as bearers of the tradition on the jubilee land laws. Renato Poggioli shows that pastoral poetry often creates a legendary past or a golden age when justice worked automatically and the weak did not

1. J.D. Levenson, *Sinai and Zion: An Entry into the Jewish Bible* (Minneapolis, MN: Winston Press, 1985), p. 18.

2. G.E. Mendenhall, 'Social Organization in Early Israel', in F. Moore Cross, W.E. Lemke and P.D. Miller, Jr (eds.), *Magnalia Dei: The Mighty Acts of God* (Garden City, NY: Doubleday, 1976), p. 140.

3. Klein, *Israel in Exile*, p. 147.

4. See Newsome, *By the Waters of Babylon*, p. 101.

fear the ravages of the powerful.[1] In the case of the priests (who were not pastoralists), the golden age was not so much one in which moral goodness prevailed but that time when the proper moral imperatives were given to the people. Once again, it was Sinai that became the focus for this legendary history, and the people were to look back to that past to gain the proper moral values for living in the contemporary situation.[2] The jubilee land laws, which in some form were already a part of the people's tradition, were also located at Sinai to help legitimate this socially reform-minded legislation in the new age.[3] The very use of the concept of patrimonial land served 'to link the generations of exile to the most formative and fundamental images of Israel's memory'.[4] The priests held before the people a moral tradition— hardly observed previously—of a relatively egalitarian distribution of land that resisted latifundism.

In addition to transmitting this moral tradition, the priests also sacralized it. The priestly level of redaction of Leviticus 25 not only clarified its commands and brought urgency to them, it also expressed the theological warrants for the law.[5] Although much of the material in the Holiness Code could be considered civil rather than sacral, the recurring refrain, 'I am the Lord your God', emphasizes the presence of God in all the matters discussed in the code, thus sacralizing all these issues.[6] In addition, the grounding of the release laws of Leviticus 25 in the exodus links the jubilee with Israel's sacred history. Eli Ginzberg believes that the theological warrants were meant to increase the likelihood that the jubilee and sabbatical regulations would be observed since they had not been in the pre-exilic period.[7] With Leviticus 26 explaining that the exile functioned as a 'forced'

1. R. Poggioli, 'Naboth's Vineyard or the Pastoral View of the Social Order', *Journal of the History of Ideas* 24 (1963), pp. 3-24.

2. See Porter, *Leviticus*, p. 3; and von Waldow, 'Social Responsibility', p. 204.

3. Gnuse, 'Jubilee Legislation in Leviticus', p. 47.

4. W. Brueggemann, *The Land* (Overtures to Biblical Theology; Philadelphia: Fortress Press, 1977), p. 143.

5. H.G. Reventlow, *Das Heiligkeitsgesetz: Formgeschichtlich Untersacht* (Neukirchen: Neukirchener Verlag, 1961), p. 130.

6. G.J. Wenham, *The Book of Leviticus* (Grand Rapids: Eerdmans, 1979), p. 17.

7. E. Ginzberg, 'Studies in the Economics of the Bible', *JQR* 22 (1932), pp. 82-83, 355-56.

sabbatical for the land—a sabbatical the people failed to observe previously—it does appear that the priests were arguing that the jubilee was not merely a civil responsibility but also a sacred obligation.

But what was the nature of that obligation? Regardless of the arguments that the covenant is a late concept, it certainly existed by the exilic period, and the priests would have become familiar with it. However, the term is rarely used in P, and it is most prominently used with regard to Noah. (Cf. Ezekiel who refers to a new, everlasting covenant [37.26].) Porter argues that P takes for granted the covenantal relationship between Israel and Yahweh as well as the prophetic proclamations regarding that relationship.[1] Kornfeld goes on to say that the formula 'I am the Lord your God' expresses a special interest in the concept of covenant.[2] This formula does present one half of the classic statement of the covenant, but if covenant is taken broadly to mean a relationship that bonds two parties in mutual responsibility, then some form of covenant clearly underlies P. There is the continual assertion that Yahweh is the God of Israel, and that assertion is presented as a warrant for ethical behavior, that is, the people are obligated to an ethical code because of their responsibility to their deity. Thus, the very existence of theological warrants for the jubilee implies the tradition of a covenant between Yahweh and Israel—a tradition transmitted by the priests to strengthen the moral force of the jubilee.

It ought also to be noted that these bearers of the tradition did not leave it unchanged. Ginzberg lists four compromises the priests made to make compliance with the jubilee law easier.[3] First, assuming the jubilee to be originally based upon the sabbatical year, Ginzberg argues that the priests lengthened the jubilee period from seven to fifty years, softening the economic impact of the land redistribution and the release of slaves. Secondly, the jubilee no longer cancelled debts as the Deuteronomic sabbatical had done. Thirdly, the jubilee no longer included a third-year tithe for the poor and the Levites. Fourthly, the priests exempted urban dwellings from the jubilee release of property. The first three items presuppose that the jubilee was part of the same tradition that appears in Exodus 32 and

1. Porter, *Leviticus*, p. 9.
2. W. Kornfeld, *Das Buch Leviticus*, Die Welt der Bibel: Kleincommentare zur Heiligen Schrift (Düsseldorf: Patmos, 1972), p. 12.
3. Ginzberg, 'Economics of the Bible', p. 389.

Deuteronomy 15. A continuous connection is difficult to prove, but there is a close enough correspondence that the differences between Leviticus 25 and the other two texts must be considered significant; the priests were formulating traditions about release and land use in a new way. The fourth item is clearly an internal compromise to deal with a particular reality. The priests did not slavishly pass on the tradition exactly as they had received it, but they used the tradition to explain the present and the future.

Explainers of the Cosmos

One of the ways the jubilee tradition was used to explain the presently existing world was to account for the exile. Berger and Luckmann describe two methods of dealing with deviations from the symbolic universe.[1] First, a society may simply deny the credibility of the deviation, thus destroying its power to delegitimate the social world. However, the exile was an event of too great proportions to deny its credibility; it was a monumental fact contradicting the popular Yahwism linked to the Davidic dynasty and Jerusalem. The priests (and others) were forced to use Berger and Luckmann's second method—the incorporation of the deviation into the symbolic universe, turning it into an affirmation. As stated above, Lev. 26.41-43 interprets the exile as an enforced sabbath, making up for the sabbaths that had not been observed previously. (We might assume that if the sabbaths were not being observed, neither were the jubilee years.) The existence of the jubilee law, which had not been observed, explained the present condition of the world in a way that maintained the integrity of Yahwism.

In addition, the jubilee tradition expressed a heightened sense of monotheism. During the exile the belief in Yahweh as the parochial God of Israel who was in conflict with other national gods was giving way to a belief in Yahweh as the one, omnipotent God of all the world. This movement may be seen most artfully in Deutero-Isaiah. The levitical institutionalization of the divine ownership of land and people was a reflection of this increasing monotheism which placed all things under God's sovereignty.[2] Thus, the priests were describing a world in which there was only one God, who had direct control of all life; therefore,

1. Berger and Luckmann, *The Social Construction of Reality*, pp. 105-107.
2. Ginzberg, 'Economics of the Bible', p. 379.

it was impossible to believe that Israel's God had been defeated by other powers. On the other hand, in such a world, the people could have hope that redemption was not only possible but certain.

Projectors of the Future

One of the most important needs a comprehensible universe meets is the ability to project the future. If the cosmos no longer functions according to the laws of society's symbolic universe, it becomes impossible to predict what may happen, and the future becomes as chaotic as the present. As the priests reconstructed the Yahwistic world, they also began to project a future based on that world—a future that would give predictability to their lives. The power elite, of whom the priests had been a part, had linked Israel's theological existence to possession of the land under the leadership of the Davidic dynasty centered in Jerusalem. Since those conditions no longer existed, either Israel as a religious community would pass out of existence, or a new foundation for its existence had to be posited. In choosing the latter option, the priests' basic affirmation of the future was that the presence of God would bring to fulfillment the ancient divine promises to Noah and the patriarchs through the cultic system given at Sinai.[1] Therefore, the future did not depend on a political system or a geographical location, but on a promise that could not be negated by any historical event.

This does not mean that the priests turned Israel into a spiritualized community that had no real social order in the everyday world. The fulfillment of that 'non-negatable' divine promise was to be actualized in the material world; therefore, the fulfillment was not to be found in the exile. A conquest narrative is lacking in P because the conquest tradition has been incorporated into the existing material in a subdued fashion since the conquest that would mark the fulfillment of the promise is still in the future.[2] Ackroyd points out that although many of the laws of the priestly material antedate the exile and come from different sources, Leviticus 26 reveals the purpose of compiling the

---

1.   Klein, *Israel in Exile*, p. 125. See also the review of G. Chr. Macholz, 'Israel und das Land: Vorarbeiten zu einem Vergleich zwischen Priesterschrift und Deuteronomistischem Geschichtswerk' (inaugural dissertation, Heidelberg, 1969) in P. Diepold, *Israels Land* (Stuttgart: Kohlhammer, 1972), pp. 7-8.

2.   Brueggemann, 'Kerygma of the Priestly Writers', p. 111.

laws, namely, to lay the foundation for the possibility of a new
community.[1] In addition, the jubilee land laws show that the new
community could not be located just anywhere; Yahweh's people
would inhabit the land given to their ancestors and bequeathed to them
through the generations. Thus, the priests still looked for a community
with its own social integrity located in the land of promise, but they
held that hope within a reconstructed Yahwistic world which was less
susceptible to negation.

There are several theories regarding what aspect of community life
the priests wished to affect by including the jubilee land laws. One
possibility is that it was intended to ensure an equal place in the new
community for impoverished exiles returning to their homeland.[2]
Gerhard Wallis states that the story of Elimelech and Naomi is a better
parallel of the jubilee legislation than that of Jeremiah's purchase of
his cousin's land because the former story deals with one who has left
the homeland, lost his property and has no legal right to it.[3] Wallis
goes on to argue that the jubilee legislation actually presupposes the
exilic situation in which people were separated from the land without
any possibility of regaining it, and it seeks a solution to the problems
that would arise when they returned to their homeland. For the
returning exiles there would be no 'redeemers' (cf. Naomi who had
Boaz) or no king to whom they could appeal (cf. the Shunamite
woman [2 Kgs 8.1-8]); therefore, new forms of regaining the land had
to be developed. Wallis concludes:

> On the basis of older customs, the jubilee-year legislation governs, in its
> final effect, the adoption of the one who was separated from farm and
> family into the former relationships, making him a full citizen again.[4]

Therefore, according to this theory, the jubilee was specifically
intended to bring the exiles, who had lost their land through no fault
of their own, back into full economic (as well as social and cultic)
participation in the community.

Another possible purpose of the jubilee land laws was to influence
political power in the new community. The priests produced the con-

---

1. Ackroyd, *Exile and Restoration*, pp. 89-90.
2. Gnuse, 'Jubilee Legislation in Leviticus', p. 43.
3. G. Wallis, 'Das Jobeljahr-Gesetz, eine Novelle zum Sabbatjahr-Gestetz',
Mitteilungen des Instituts für Orientforschung 15 (1969), pp. 339-43.
4. Wallis, 'Das Jobeljahr-Gesetz', p. 341.

cept of Yahweh as the ultimate owner of the land, and that concept
would be advantageous to their quest for political and economic
power in the future.[1] We have already noted that there was a link
between land ownership and membership in the cultic community; that
linkage itself would have placed the priests in a position of great economic power with the ability to include or exclude individuals from
the cult.[2] The claim that Yahweh owned the land gave the priests even
greater power since they were the logical 'caretakers' of Yahweh's
interests.[3] As Sharon Ringe puts it:

> The new compilation [of the Holiness Code] would resolve a major
> problem accompanying the people's return from exile, namely, the allo-
> cation and subsequent management of the land. The priestly compilers of
> the laws thus would not only have established their own authority over the
> regulation of the land and its inhabitants, but at the same time would have
> legitimized their administration by a reaffirmation of its basis in God's
> sovereignty. The religious sanction that such legislation would have lent to
> their authority would have been crucial in the consolidation of their power
> and in the establishment of the holy and righteous people under God
> which was their aim.[4]

Ringe's comment moves beyond the rather cynical accusation of the
priests making a naked power play. If the jubilee tended to give the
priests more leverage in economic policy, it also strengthened the
religious leadership of the priests, moving the projected new community in the direction of a 'holy nation'.

If it is naive to ignore the priests' worldly quest for power, it is also
overly cynical to discount the truly religious motivations of the priests
to produce a single, righteous community. Arndt Meinhold points out
that the priestly writer who finally formed Leviticus 25 no longer
locates fraternal solidarity in belonging to a clan *(mišpaḥâ)* but in
belonging to the whole people of Israel *(bĕnê yisrā'ēl)*.[5] The
centralization of power has its risks of abuse, but it also has its potential
to unify a people. The Israelites had been a fragmented people, and

   1. E. Neufeld, 'Socio-Economic Background of Yobel and Šĕmitta', *Rivista
degli Studi Orientali* 33 (1958), p. 66.
   2. See Blenkinsopp, *History of Prophecy*, p. 228.
   3. Smith, *Palestinian Parties and Politics*, p. 108.
   4. S.H. Ringe, *Jesus, Liberation, and the Biblical Jubilee: Images for Ethics
and Christology* (Philadelphia: Fortress Press, 1985), pp. 26-27.
   5. A. Meinhold, 'Zur Beziehung Gott, Volk, Land im Jobel-Zusammenhang',
BZ 29 (1985), pp. 258-59.

their fragmentation caused much suffering among God's people. Now
the priests sought a way to create a new community in which all the
people would be linked to each other in mutual responsibility and care
under Yahweh's leadership. The priestly projection was not a vision
of a future age in which humanity would be perfected—the jubilee
was meant to correct the constant imperfections—but a belief in a
stable cosmic constitution which can, and must, be obeyed.[1]

Summary

As a significant group within the intelligentsia of the shattered
Israelite community, the priests had the monumental task of rescuing
the Yahwistic world-view from total negation and reinterpreting it in
light of the contemporary situation. They transplanted the source of
that world-view's legitimation to a more secure location—that is,
Sinai rather than Zion—and revived Israel's moral traditions basing
them in that new source. In passing along these revised traditions, they
stabilized the universe and were able to project a viable future for the
Yahwistic community. Indeed, it was the priests' most important
function to envision the re-establishment of a community following
the punishment of the exile, a community whose social policy was to
be so well founded on the Sinai traditions that the apostacy and injustice
that led to the exile would not be repeated.[2] Like most mortals, the
priests' motives were a mixture of religious high-mindedness and self-
interest; however, the jubilee tradition they reinterpreted and handed
on has a life and meaning of its own, which will be thoroughly explored
in Part III.

---

1. Eichrodt, *Theology of the Old Testament*, II, p. 174.
2. See Brueggemann, 'The Kerygma of the Priestly Writers', pp. 103-105, 112.

Chapter 5

EZEKIEL

Introduction

The purpose of this section is to examine how a world-view which is related to, yet distinct from, the priestly one, handles the question of land tenure. This comparison and contrast will help pinpoint the meaning of the jubilee land laws by emphasizing some of its aspects and clarifying the boundaries of others. Throughout this section, the name Ezekiel will be attached to the text being studied, but the referent of that name will be discussed below in the examination of the authorship of this text; 'Ezekiel' is being used as a matter of convenience, not as referring to the prophet himself. However, both the canonical location of this text and scholarly opinion indicate that this is not an arbitrary nomenclature, as will be clarified below.

Whether one considers Leviticus 25 to be a part of the Holiness Code or the priestly work, there is a clear correspondence between it and Ezekiel. Both Ezekiel and the Holiness Code place a great deal of stress on holiness, which is the main point of connection between the two works.[1] How and if the two influenced each other is a more difficult matter to explain. This is a complicated issue because both works were undergoing literary development at approximately the same time; therefore, certain materials in the Holiness Code might have influenced the prophet, who in turn influenced later additions to H, which in turn influenced later editors of Ezekiel. The one literary connection between Ezekiel and Leviticus 25 is Ezekiel's reference to a 'year of release' (46.16-18), which presupposes the jubilee regulations. The allusion is so casual that it appears that Ezekiel assumed familiarity with the concept; thus, the jubilee (or that which underlies the written laws of Leviticus 25) worked its way into Ezekiel. What

1. Ackroyd, *Exile and Restoration*, p. 88.

can be said is that the circles which produced the Holiness Code must have been relatively close to the circles that produced Ezekiel.[1]

There is some evidence of the chronological priority of Ezekiel to the priestly work, but the literary and theological relationships are ambiguous. As in the case of the Holiness Code, Ezekiel and P were developing during the exile, and the circles producing these two works were related. I shall examine in more detail how Ezekiel was related to the priestly circle that produced P.

The Text of Chapters 40–48

I begin by examining the final section of the book of Ezekiel, which is quite different in form and content from chs. 1–39. Although the differences are very apparent, this final section is not unrelated to the rest of the book. This section is structurally necessary for the whole book, particularly in balancing the vision of the departure of God's glory from the defiled temple in chs. 8–11.[2] Ackroyd connects the two major parts of the book by noting a natural progression from one to the other; Ezekiel 33–37 provides 'the general principles of restoration', chs. 38–39 expresses the 'epitome of the overthrow of the evil powers' and chs. 40–48 provides a detailed description of the divine restoration as it actually will be effected in the future.[3] Besides this structural connection to the rest of the book, placing chs. 40–48 squarely within the 'Ezekielian' tradition, it has its own internal structure. Haran sees three simple subsections: 40.1–44.3 is a description of the temple form, 44.4–46.24 prescribes the temple procedures and 47–48 describes and allots the land.[4] It is this last subsection in which we are most interested.

Authorship and Date

The question of authorship and date is important for a full understanding of how Ezekiel's description of land distribution might compare and contrast with the jubilee legislation. I shall begin

1. W. Zimmerli, *Ezekiel* (2 vols.; Hermeneia; Philadelphia: Fortress Press, 1983), I, p. 52.

2. S. Talmon and M. Fishbane, 'The Structuring of Biblical Books: Studies in the Book of Ezekiel', *ASTI* 10 (1976), p. 139; Zimmerli, *Ezekiel*, p. 327.

3. Ackroyd, *Exile and Restoration*, pp. 110-11.

4. M. Haran, 'The Law Code of Ezekiel XL-XLVIII and its Relation to the Priestly School', *HUCA* 50 (1979), p. 43.

answering that question by forming a hypothesis about the date of 47.13–48.29. Clearly, the major theme of the entire last section of the book is the restoration of Jerusalem and the nation. May takes this to be characteristic of a later editor who added this section to the book in the early fifth century.[1] That is to say that May takes the discussion of the restoration as descriptive of events that had taken place (or were taking place) or as normative for what the editor thought should be taking place. However, the text purports to be predictive, and there is no evidence to contradict that. Indeed the entire section—and most particularly the description of the land allotments—is so schematic that it probably ought not to be taken as descriptive *or* normative. Von Rad considers that fact as an argument for its late date, comparing it with Zech. 14.10 as a proto-apocalyptic vision of an elevated new Jerusalem.[2] As we shall see below, this material may be taken as utopian, but that does not imply a postexilic date; many of the prophecies of Deutero-Isaiah look toward a restoration of the people that is unrealistic in actual history.

Regarding the entire last section of the book, Howie believes that the great detail of the description of the east gate and its correspondence with the plan for Solomonic gates imply that chs. 40–48 were written by someone who has seen that gate before the temple's destruction.[3] It is possible that drawings of the gate and temple survived, and a later author was able to work from them; however, such a detailed description of the gate would have been moot after the reconstruction was a *fait accompli*. Regarding the discussion of the land, Zimmerli dates the material before the fall of Babylon to Cyrus for two major reasons. The description of the boundaries of the land may be based on list documents from the pre-exilic period, but it was not produced after 538 because there is no evidence of the restoration; it is a document still looking forward to a reoccupation of the land.[4] Secondly, the description of the allotment of the land does not display any of the actual tensions associated with the return of the exiles to the

1. H.G. May, 'Ezekiel', *Interpreter's Bible* (Nashville: Abingdon Press, 1956), VI, pp. 45, 332.

2. Von Rad, *Old Testament Theology*, II, p. 296 n. 3.

3. C.G. Howie, *The Date and Composition of Ezekiel* (JBL Monograph Series, 4; Philadelphia: SBL, 1950), pp. 43-46.

4. Zimmerli, *Ezekiel*, II, p. 542.

land.[1] A distinction is made between the Zadokites and the Levites, but none of the animosity that is displayed in postexilic literature is present. Also there appears to be an assumed harmony under the leadership of 'the prince'—a harmony that was never realized under the governors of the Judean province. There is a powerful enough hope in a return to the homeland that a detailed description of the restoration and reallotment of the land is deemed appropriate, but that restoration is still in the future; therefore, 47.13–48.29 probably dates from the late exile—contemporary with P's redaction of the jubilee land laws.

In order to corroborate this hypothesis, a closer examination needs to be made of the relationship between this unit and the prophet Ezekiel. One possibility is to assert that the whole last section of the book (chs. 40–48) comes from the prophet himself, but was connected to the rest of the book by Ezekiel's disciples after his death.[2] As we have just seen, the structure of that final section suggests multiple authorship, but if one allows for later additions in a work that is predominantly from the prophet, this hypothesis cannot be ruled out. Fohrer points out that after 585 Ezekiel himself shifts his prophetic message to one of hope in the redemption of the people and the return of Yahweh to the land.[3] Although the form is very different in chs. 40–48, the content is quite compatible with the prophet's views of salvation found in the first part of the book. May reminds us that Ezekiel was also a priest and a Zadokite, facts which would explain the emphasis on cultic matters and a preference for the Zadokites in chs. 40–48; however, he does not include the passage on which we are focused (47.13–48.19) among those that can be attributed to Ezekiel himself.[4] Haran believes that the visions within Ezekiel 40–48 come directly from his prophetic imagination, while the laws derive from the priestly heritage, the two being adapted into a single prophetic/priestly literary composition.[5] Once Haran has made such a distinction, the question arises whether substantial portions of chs. 40–48 (including 47.13–48.29) actually come from another hand.

Zimmerli believes that the description of the borders and the land allotments was originally extra-prophetic legal material that was

1. Zimmerli, *Ezekiel*, II, p. 553.
2. Howie, *Date and Composition of Ezekiel*, pp. 99-102.
3. Fohrer, *History of Israelite Religion*, p. 318.
4. May, 'Ezekiel', pp. 53-54.
5. Haran, 'The Law Code of Ezekiel 40–48', pp. 50-53.

incorporated in Ezekiel with little change and cannot be attributed to
the prophet himself.[1] May describes the one who added this material
to Ezekiel as an editor,[2] but who was this editor and how did he make
his decisions? Although some of the material in chs. 40–48 is at odds
with that of chs. 1–39, the prophet might have authored some of the
fundamental sections, and all these chapters were formed by 'a kind of
Ezekielian "school" ', which worked in accordance with the prophet's
own theology.[3] Therefore, even though the redactional complexity of
the book is very high, all the ideas found in it conform to an Ezekiel
tradition that was based on the prophet's own work. Ackroyd adds
that this means that all the material connected to the name Ezekiel has
a narrow theological focus and socio-historical context.[4] Thus, even if
the regulations concerning land distribution did not come from the
prophet himself, they do fit within a narrow theological and socio-
historical circle centered on Ezekiel. A description of that circle is
crucial for our comparative analysis.

Social Location of 'Ezekiel'

The first thing that can be said about the Ezekielian school's close
adherence to the prophet's visions is that it envisioned a theocratic
community 'centered around the temple and its priesthood'.[5] Within
the description of the land allotment, the majority of the space is
devoted to a detailed delineation of the *tĕrûmâ*, the sacred area set
aside for the temple and 'protected' by the priests and Levites from
contamination. Even the purpose of 'the city' (obviously Jerusalem) is
merely to serve the physical needs of the temple and the sacrifices that
occur there. In addition, this portrayal of the land is set in the context
of Ezekiel's law code, which is almost exclusively focused on the ritual
life of the restored community. This much interest in the cult implies
that the Ezekielian school, like the prophet himself, was a part of the
priesthood and shared many of the concerns of the redactors of the

1. W. Zimmerli, *Ezekiel*, I, p. 35. See also his 'Plans for Rebuilding after the
Catastrophe of 587', in W. Brueggemann (ed.), *I Am Yahweh* (trans. D. Stott;
Atlanta: John Knox, 1984), p. 126; and Gottwald, *The Hebrew Bible*, p. 488.
2. May, 'Ezekiel', p. 53.
3. Zimmerli, 'Plans for Rebuilding', pp. 114-15.
4. Ackroyd, *Exile and Restoration*, p. 103.
5. May, 'Ezekiel', p. 54.

jubilee legislation. For both Ezekiel and P, the land was set apart by Yahweh for the sake of the people, and its distribution was a matter of religious concern, not civil.

We have already noted that this material comes from the exilic period. The destruction of Judah had nearly eliminated the Jews' entire social structure. There were still priests, many of them in exile, and traditional social functions continued, but in large measure the exile presented the Jews with a 'clean slate' on which to produce a new social order with radically different relationships among the groups in the community and radically different functions for those groups to perform.[1] Since it appears that Ezekiel was part of the priesthood, the prophet and his school were also part of the intelligentsia who faced the pressures created by the exile and its 'clean slate'. On the one hand, Ezekiel was faced with explaining the exile in the first place. Ezekiel was very concerned to prove that the disaster of 587 was the just punishment of that generation for its own sin; thus the exile did not delegitimate the rule of Yahweh.[2] On the other hand, Ezekiel was also concerned to make the people learn from the apostasy in Israel's history and look forward to redemption and the restoration of the community.[3] Like P, Ezekiel was engaged in the task of sustaining the Yahwistic world and creating a constitution for a new community that would avoid the problems of the old one.

Besides these similarities between Ezekiel and the priestly writers, there are also two very important differences. First, the regulations presented in Ezekiel 40–48 (including those regarding the land) are among the few laws not founded upon the Sinai event. Despite some differences between the priestly laws and the laws of the Ezekiel code, it is clear that the legislation in Ezekiel is based on the same traditions as that in P. Ezekiel was probably not a legal innovator, yet Ezekiel does not attempt to legitimate the laws by placing the source of their legitimacy in the sacred past. Ezekiel does not refer to great historical locations or holy persons of old in claiming the prescriptive power of the laws, rather these laws come through direct divine revelation to Ezekiel the prophet. Of course, his disciples attributed laws to Ezekiel, a holy man from the past, but he was one from the recent

1.   See Zimmerli, 'Plans for Rebuilding', p. 126; Howie, *Date and Composition of Ezekiel*, p. 84.

2.   Ackroyd, *Exile and Restoration*, pp. 106-10.

3.   May, 'Ezekiel', p. 62.

past, either still living or personally known to some who were still living. Thus, the Ezekiel community did not rely on history for the legitimacy of their claims, even though the content of those claims came from their ancestors. Some of what the predecessors had handed down to them was worth saving, but nothing in their history was able to legitimize it.

The reliance on divine revelation points to the second important difference. Ezekiel, who was a member of the priestly caste and was primarily concerned with cultic matters, has been labelled a 'prophet'. Priests are those persons who carry out the rituals that were founded in the dim past and carry authority because of their antiquity. The nature of priesthood requires a sacred past when the laws regulating the cultic life of the people were given by the deity to a particular group of persons who would be eternally responsible for the cult. Ezekiel did not fit this mold. Ezekiel received a particular call to proclaim the word of Yahweh which was revealed specifically to him at that time. Although it was not much different from the word written by the priests, Ezekiel claimed that the word he proclaimed was uniquely legitimate because it was received directly from God.

This leads to the hypothesis that Ezekiel and his disciples were priests for whom the mainline priestly legitimations of the Yahwistic world were inadequate. The priests recognized the need for a reinterpretation of the roots of the Yahwistic community, but they were conservative and kept those roots deeply planted in Israel's history—even deeper than the old Davidic legitimations. Apparently for Ezekiel, the exile had called into question all of Israel's history; therefore, a radical change had to be made in the way Yahwism was to be defended. Thus, Ezekiel broke with the mainline priestly faction and formed a priestly group that existed at the fringe of the priesthood. It might be said that the book of Ezekiel comprises a 'minority report' of the priestly world-view; it is priestly in its focus and much of its content, but it is based on a different view of why these things are as they are.

The Distribution of Land

Now we must examine how this view from the fringe understood land and its distribution. Much of Ezek. 47.13–48.29 indicates that this material is based on ancient traditions. The delineation of the boundary leaves out the territory east of the Jordan, thus making the boundaries of the land conform more closely with the territory promised to the patriarchs. It may be that the Transjordan, not being part of the promised land, was considered polluted or in some way unfit for Israelite settlement.[1] Abraham made clear to his servant that Isaac must remain in the Cisjordan, the land given to him by Yahweh (Gen. 24.6-8). In addition, the inclusion of Philistine and Phoenician territories within the boundaries of Israel follows an old tradition of the ideal extent of the promised land (cf. Gen. 9.18-27 and Judg. 1.31).[2] Comparing the boundaries given in 47.15-20 to other models in the Hebrew Bible, Yehezkel Kaufmann concludes that they define the land promised to the patriarchs rather than Moses' land, Joshua's land, the land actually settled or the land of the political entity of Israel.[3] Thus, the geographical area to comprise the restored community will conform to the ancient promise.

There are enough similarities between Ezekiel's description of the borders and other boundary lists, especially that of Num. 34.1-12, that it seems likely that they rest on common traditions.[4] Eichrodt notes that the southern boundary is not a straight line from west to east, but bends far to the south to include the oasis of Kadesh, which has its association with Moses.[5] This is another example of Ezekiel's using the content of tradition while abandoning its legitimating function. A tradition—which the mainline priests connected to Moses at Sinai and whose very content could remind one of Moses' leadership of the Yahwistic community—was presented as a revelation just received from God by Ezekiel. If these associations with Moses were not so subtle as to be missed, they might have served a legitimating function themselves—unspoken allusions to the authority of the lawgiver.

---

1.   See J.D. Levenson, *Theology of the Program of Restoration of Ezekiel 40–48* (Missoula, MT: Scholars Press, 1976), p. 115; W. Eichrodt, *Ezekiel* (OTL; Philadelphia: Westminster Press, 1970), pp. 590-91; Zimmerli, *Ezekiel*, II, p. 531.

2.   Zimmerli, *Ezekiel*, II, pp. 531-32.

3.   Zimmerli, *Ezekiel*, II, pp. 529-30.

4.   See H. Gese (*Verfassungsentwurf des Ezekiel (Kap. 40-48) traditionsgeschichtlich Untersucht* [Beiträge zur historichen Theologie, 25; Tübingen: Mohr, 1957], p. 99) who notes that the differences are great enough that one cannot claim direct dependency; and May, 'Ezekiel', p. 329. Zimmerli suggests that the use of *nhl* in connection with settlement is paralleled in the earlier settlement traditions (*Ezekiel*, II, p. 528).

5   Eichrodt, *Ezekiel*, p. 591.

There is yet another connection between Ezekiel's discussion of land distribution and Israel's tradition. The narrative of Joshua 22, a part of the occupation history, expresses the concern that the land east of the Jordan did not belong to Yahweh and therefore was unclean.[1] Thus, the tradition of Israel's occupation of the land contributed to the rejection of the Transjordan as part of the restored nation. The nature of the allocation of the land described by Ezekiel appears to be a typology rooted in the original distribution of tribal lands under Joshua.[2] The very fact that the land is to be allotted to tribes recalls the period preceding the bureaucratic divisions of the monarchy, the period of the peasant tribal confederation.[3] The center of the land is the temple not the palace or even Jerusalem (the civil capital), and the one responsible for the leadership in the civil life of the community is a 'prince' not a king, again reminiscent of the period of the judges and theocratic rule.[4] According to Ezekiel, the Yahwistic community is not to be restored in a new land but the land promised and given to the ancestors and handed down through the generations. This in itself adds legitimacy to Ezekiel's claims, but Ezekiel makes little of this historical continuity and the details of the vision break sharply with historical reality.

As just noted, the tribal structure used in 48.1-29 (a structure almost totally missing in the rest of Ezekiel and in Deutero-Isaiah) is a way to look back to the original settlement and pass over the era when the tribes were dissolved. Besides a return to an era in Israel's sacred past, this reversion to tribal allotments may be a criticism of the administrative districts first produced by Solomon.[5] The very layout of the tribes may be an attempt to avoid the problems created by the monarchy. Levenson suggests that Judah is allotted land to the north of Jerusalem and Benjamin to the south in order to prevent the favoritism

1.   G. von Rad, 'The Promised Land and Yahweh's Land in the Hexateuch', in *The Problem of the Hexateuch and Other Essays* (trans. E.W. Trueman Dicken; London: SCM Press, 1984), p. 87.

2.   Brueggemann, *The Land*, p. 142.

3.   See W. Zimmerli, *The Old Testament and the World* (Atlanta: John Knox, 1976), p. 74; Levenson, *Program of Restoration*, p. 112; M. Noth, 'The Laws in the Pentateuch', in *The Laws in the Pentateuch and Other Studies* (London: SCM Press, 1984), pp. 68-69.

4.   Levenson, *Program of Restoration*, pp. 111-12.

5.   Klein, *Israel in Exile*, pp. 90-91.

enjoyed by the south during the monarchy.[1] In addition, the Levites
are placed between the temple precinct and Judah in order to reverse
the former monarchical blurring of sacred and secular when the
palace and temple precincts adjoined each other.[2] Ezekiel's careful
avoidance of speaking of a king may be just one more way to express
a critique of the power of the monarchy and the abuses of that power
which led to the destruction of the nation. P shifted the source of the
legitimation for the Yahwistic community away from the monarchy,
but it did not criticize the existence of the monarchy. Ezekiel took the
more radical course, and suggested the end of the monarchy altogether.

This critique of the monarchy is echoed in a shift in the status of
Jerusalem. Levenson argues that the arrangement of the tribes places
Jerusalem at the center of the restored land, at the navel of the earth,
the source of all existence.[3] However, it is the temple that is at the
actual center of the *tĕrûmâ*, and 'the city' appears to be a mere adjunct
to the temple. Jerusalem becomes secularized, dividing it from the
holy precinct (that is, palace from temple), and populated by workers
from all the tribes; thus, it is no longer the private domain of the king
who mixed the affairs of state with the affairs of the cult.[4] It is
significant that, even though it is Jerusalem that is referred to in this
section, Ezekiel never names it. Perhaps a section for Jerusalem was
set aside next to the temple precinct within the 25,000 cubit square in
the middle of the land as a concession to the long tradition of the association between Jerusalem and the temple.[5] In addition, the temple and
cult envisioned by Ezekiel would require a large number of people to
maintain them, and the presence of these people would imply the presence of a city. The center of the cosmos would be the temple and only
the temple.

Of even greater departure from tradition is Ezekiel's inclusion of
the *gērîm* in the allotment of the land. The prescription giving the
gērîm a share in the patrimony 'is much more radical than anything
else in all the legal corpora of the Hebrew Bible'.[6] Nowhere else are
non-Israelites given such security as this. Yet it echoes the priestly

1. Levenson, *Program of Restoration*, p. 118.
2. Levenson, *Program of Restoration*, p. 119.
3. Levenson, *Sinai and Zion*, p. 119.
4. Klein, *Israel in Exile*, p. 92.
5. Zimmerli, 'Plans for Rebuilding', p. 128.
6. Levenson, *Program of Restoration*, p. 123.

emphasis on the sacral character of those who dwell on the land as opposed to Israelites per se (cf. Lev. 17.15-16).[1] May argues that *gērîm* here refers to proselytes (as it does in later sources), pointing out that the Septuagint interprets it as such.[2] Even if the *gērîm* had to be proselytes to Yahwism in order to share in the land distribution, the inclusion of non-Israelites in the community of Yahweh worshippers is new to the exile and a radical departure from the pre-exilic period.[3] Ezekiel's vision took a major step in separating Yahwism from an ethnic group. The Israelites were still the chosen people, to be sure; however, in Ezekiel's notion of a Yahwistic world, the group known as 'Israelites' and the group known as 'Yahweh's people' were not identical. The mainline priests may have shared this belief in general, but Ezekiel made it concrete.

The aspect of Ezekiel's description of the allotment of the land that most clearly displays the radical repudiation of the monarchical world-view is the utopian nature of the vision.[4] There are several aspects of Ezekiel's vision of the restored land that display a utopian unreality. First, by the time of the exile, the division of the people by tribes had been lost.[5] Genealogical lists may have allowed persons to know to which family they belonged, but the geographical distinctions among the tribes had vanished. In addition, those tribes which had lived in the north disappeared in the Assyrian exile and no longer existed. Besides, if an ancient attachment to particular locations had survived, it would be impossible to rearrange those attachments arbitrarily as Ezekiel did in the tribal allotments.

Secondly, the boundaries established by Ezekiel could not exist in historical reality. The southern boundary was set at Meribath-kadesh and the northern at the entrance of the *biga* in defiance of political

---

1. Levenson, *Program of Restoration*, p. 123.
2. May, 'Ezekiel', p. 331.
3. Zimmerli, *Ezekiel, II*, p. 532; 'Plans for Rebuilding', p. 129.
4. Mannheim points out that when one's own social setting is not satisfying, one constructs other places and other periods which do conform to one's own world-view. Mannheim calls such a construction a 'utopia' and says that a utopian vision reorders all of life so that even the past is given meaning in accordance with the vision (*Ideology and Utopia*, pp. 205-10). What we would call 'objective reality' becomes secondary to the vision so that a world is constructed that could not possibly exist in the empirical world.
5. Zimmerli, *Ezekiel*, II, p. 541.

reality.[1] Haran claims that the description of the boundary in Ezekiel must be based on a literary memory since those boundaries had not existed in reality since Canaan was an Egyptian province.[2] I have already noted that these borders seem to correspond to the land promised to the patriarchs, so the area of the restored land conformed to an ideal rather than an entity that might actually come into existence. The internal boundaries also betray an unreality. Zimmerli believes that the *îš kĕ'āḥîw* of 47.14 may indicate that the north–south measurements of the tribal allotments are to be identical.[3] Such a method of distributing the land, if carried out literally, would hardly provide equal shares for each tribe, yet that appears to be Ezekiel's intention. If these highly schematic internal borders are to express the equality Ezekiel intends, they must be taken as part of a utopian vision that does not correspond to the objective world.

Thirdly, I have noted that the rearrangement of the geographical positions of the tribes is a rather remarkable imposition on tradition, even if the tribes no longer inhabited those areas.[4] Yet even that rearrangement had a purpose in displaying the utopia envisioned by Ezekiel. In spite of the presumed equality of the allotments, there is still a hierarchy of status among the tribes. Those tribes that tradition assigns to the servants Bilhah and Zilpah are given areas farthest from the temple reflecting their lower status.[5] This arrangement also serves to emphasize the centrality of the temple in the life of the community; those tribes with higher status have easier accessibility to the locus of their cult. In fact, Zebulon and Issachar are moved to the south in order to place the temple more in the center of the land, 'as befits the "navel of the earth"'.[6] That the temple precinct is somewhat south of the literal center is a slight concession to geographical reality, but all other historical and geographical considerations are disregarded in Ezekiel's utopia.[7]

Fourthly, this unrealistic geography looks toward an idealistic society. Ralph Klein says of Ezekiel's land distribution scheme:

1. Zimmerli, 'Plans for Rebuilding', pp. 126-27.
2. Haran, 'The Law Code of Ezekiel 40–48', pp. 60-61.
3. Zimmerli, *Ezekiel*, II, p. 533.
4. See also Zimmerli, *Ezekiel*, II, p. 541.
5. Levenson, *Program of Restoration*, p. 117.
6. Levenson, *Program of Restoration*, p. 118.
7. Eichrodt, *Ezekiel*, p. 593.

The map's division into twelve tribal allotments and a central sacred area
symbolizes God's saving intent; it is not a realistic blueprint...Perhaps we
should see here a reaffirmation of the egalitarian principles of early Israel,
according to which all things really belong to Yahweh and no one was to
accumulate riches at the expense of his neighbor.[1]

As already discussed, Ezekiel's allotment of the land to the tribes echoes
the assignment of tribal territories by Joshua after the conquest.[2]
However, the restoration of the Yahwistic community under a foreign
empire's control would be very different from the creation of an auton-
omous confederation of tribes (whether such a confederation was a historical reality or not). The society that Ezekiel envisioned was a society
that could not exist within the realities of an ancient Middle East
dominated by Babylonia or Persia. But Ezekiel was creating a utopia,
another place and another period that conformed to his world-view.

Finally, Ezekiel's utopianism may be found in the date of the entire
vision. The reference in 40.1 to the twenty-fifth year (one half of
fifty) and the tenth day of the month at the beginning of the year, may
allude to Leviticus 25, making the entire vision of the restoration a
reference to the hope in a 'year of release'.[3] Indeed, the number
twenty-five is very prominent in the temple vision; all the dimensions
of the buildings in the temple precinct are multiples of twenty-five.[4]
To be at the midpoint of a jubilee cycle was to have 'turned the corner'
and to be moving in the direction of renewal. Ezekiel makes a direct
reference to the year of release in 46.17 so it is clear that Ezekiel held
a notion of a set period when conditions of imbalance where rectified.
Whether Ezekiel is referring to Leviticus 25 or the concept of such a
year that happens to occur every 50 years is unimportant; Ezekiel's
vision of the restoration of the land is related to the notion that, because
the land actually belongs to Yahweh, it cannot be permanently alienated
from those for whom Yahweh intended it. For Ezekiel, the time of
renewal would come on schedule regardless of historical realities.

Implications

There are certain implications of Ezekiel's land distribution that need

1.   Klein, *Israel in Exile*, p. 90.
2.   See also Blenkinsopp, *History of Prophecy*, p. 205.
3.   Zimmerli, 'Das "gnadenjahr des Herrn" ', p. 329.
4.   Klein, *Israel in Exile,* p. 93 n. 25.

to be examined. The use of the word *těrûmâ* to describe the central portion of the land is an indication that part of the land itself, as well as its fruit, is to be set aside as a tribute to Yahweh.[1] Yahweh is the actual sovereign of the land and, as such, is entitled to 'royal' lands and their produce as acknowledgment of that sovereignty. However, it is not the case that the people are presenting God with a portion of their land as a gift, rather, the section reserved for holy purposes is a concrete manifestation of the belief that Yahweh is the real owner of all the land, and the partitioning of the land among the tribes is a divine gift.[2] This setting aside a portion of the land as sacred is parallel to the setting aside of a portion of one's produce or the setting aside of one year in seven to let the land lie fallow. All of these actions remind the people that everything belongs to Yahweh who grants them the right to reap the benefits of the land.[3] If Yahweh's land is allotted equally among the tribes, there is the implication that it is God's intent for all persons to enjoy an equal share in the blessings of the land; therefore, the Yahwistic community ought to be about the task of maintaining that equality.

Ezekiel's distribution of the land also implies a weakening of the central political authority. The 'prince' of chs. 40–48 is the most distinguished member of the congregation, but he is excluded from any priestly function, and his palace is separated from the temple.[4] This strips the political leader of any religious power and keeps the religious community independent of civil control, thus preventing many of the cultic abuses (and the concomitant abuses of power) that occurred under the pre-exilic kings. Ezekiel's use of *naśi* recalls the premonarchic image of Israel's rulers who led the people by their charisma not by their might.[5] Indeed, the prince does not have an absolute right of disposal even over his own land because God has given it to him, and the prince may not confiscate others' land because God has given it to them.[6] In a feudal system, the sovereign may repossess land that had been given to an individual, but since Yahweh is the true owner of all the land, Israel's leader has no right to any land but that granted by

1. Zimmerli, *Ezekiel*, II, p. 533.
2. Zimmerli, 'Plans for Rebuilding', p. 127.
3. Zimmerli, *The Old Testament and the World*, p. 75.
4. Zimmerli, 'Plans for Rebuilding', pp. 124-25; Klein, *Israel in Exile*, pp. 89-90.
5. Klein, *Israel in Exile*, p. 89.
6. Zimmerli, *Ezekiel*, II, pp. 496-97.

God. In addition, the ruler's land is inalienable, to prevent him from becoming indebted and seeking others' land in order to recoup his losses.[1] In Ezekiel's world, power is held under strict control to prevent the powerful from accumulating wealth at the expense of the masses.

Finally, Ezekiel's distribution of the land implies a new age in which the kingdom of Yahweh is based on upholding the community and fulfilling the historic divine promises. The allotment of land to each tribe ensures the continued survival of that tribe as a part of Yahweh's chosen people, thus maintaining the proper structure of the congregation. In Ezekiel's vision of the restoration, the constitution of Yahweh's community is inextricably bound with the redistribution of Yahweh's land; without the proper distribution and use of the land a community reflecting Yahwistic principles is impossible.[2] The appropriate allotment of the sacred land also included a concern for justice (an issue present elsewhere in Ezekiel). The only way to honor the holy one on the sacred land is to perform the justice demanded by the owner—justice that includes the proper distribution of the land.[3] Without a just distribution of the land, the divine promises cannot be fulfilled for many of Yahweh's people because they will fall victim to the abuses of power held by the wealthy, and they will not be able to participate in the promised blessings. Ezekiel envisions a people living on the land in accordance with the knowledge that the land belongs to Yahweh.

The actualization of this just kingdom would usher in a new age. The plan to allot the land to all twelve tribes indicates that the expectation that Yahweh was about to gather all the exiles back to the homeland was about to be fulfilled.[4] The new distribution is actually a sign of the new order which not only establishes God's promises to Israel, but completely renews the life of the world (cf. 47.1-12).[5] For Ezekiel the restored community will not be simply a better version of the former community, merely purged of some problems that caused its temporary breakdown; Yahweh's community will be something different, not absolutely discontinuous from the pre-exilic community,

---

1. North, *Sociology of the Biblical Jubilee*, p. 40.
2. H. Wilderberger, 'Israel und sein Land', *EvT* 16 (1956), p. 114.
3. W. Zimmerli, *Old Testament Theology in Outline* (trans. D. Green; Edinburgh: T. & T. Clark, 1978), p. 114.
4. W. Zimmerli, *Ezekiel*, II, p. 542.
5. Ackroyd, *Exile and Restoration*, p. 251.

but something that displays a significant cosmic shift. The traditions of the ancestors will continue to exist, but those traditions will no longer bear the weight of legitimating the Yahwistic community, whose legitimacy will lie with God's redemptive act alone.

Conclusion

This chapter has been an attempt to analyze two responses to a particular social situation. These responses came from two different but closely related groups, and both dealt with the issue of land holding. There is no direct evidence of actual conflict between the two groups, but the differences in outlook between them must have led to some debate and struggle for acceptance within the community as a whole. Conflicts do arise when subgroups within society do not share the same interpretations of the past or projections of the future.[1] The mainline priests and Ezekiel did share many of the traditions of the past, but Ezekiel interpreted that past as more filled with rebellion than did the priests. Both looked toward a restored community based on Yahwistic principles, but Ezekiel's community was more radically new, involving a fundamental change in the legitimation of its existence. Do these differences mean anything? In conflicts among groups of intellectuals concerning the definition of the universe, social entities will adopt theories based on their applicability to the pragmatic interests of the social entity.[2]

Both the mainline priests and Ezekiel envisioned a theocratic state in which the priests held significant power in the central authority. However, Ezekiel's vision was more far-reaching in the change in basic social structure; it was revolutionary. Although it was, to a degree, based on Israel's traditions, Ezekiel did not use tradition as a warrant for the community he proposed because the tradition itself was fundamentally flawed and would have to be transformed. Only the direct activity of Yahweh could ground the new social structure, which bore little resemblance to the old structure (beyond the existence of a priesthood at a temple in the middle of a nation composed of twelve tribes). This is evidence of a group that was outside the power structure and whose only access to power was the overthrow of the present structure. Apparently the mainline priests maintained enough influence

1. Harrod, *The Human Center*, pp. 89-91.
2. Berger and Luckmann, *The Social Construction of Reality*, pp. 110-11.

in the exilic community that they would be the logical leaders of the restored Judea, while the Ezekiel subgroup was a fringe within the priesthood that was not going to share in the power. The Ezekiel subgroup had to rely on divine intervention to bring them to a place of influence; that is, from an Ezekielian point of view, the new age must be inaugurated and a sacred community established. In such a community, life will proceed according to the will of Yahweh; therefore, the land may be properly distributed once, and it will remain so for ever.

On the other hand, the mainline priests envisioned a community that was more contiguous with the past. Certainly, it was more theocratic than the pre-exilic nation, thus centralizing more power in the hands of the priests; however, it uses Israelite tradition as the legitimating ground of the restored nation. This indicates a group that is relatively satisfied with the social structure as it is to be established in reality. These priests anticipated enjoying a significant level of influence over the affairs of the new community, therefore no radical change was needed. The same institutions could remain; they simply needed to be purged of the flaws that tainted them and improved in order to conform more closely with true Yahwistic principles. This was not revolutionary, but progressive. In this case there was no need for a new order or a new age; the old order was adequate with some 'fine-tuning'. The jubilee did not presuppose a sacred community in which land originally distributed equally among the people would remain so, but it acknowledged the economic realities of the world and was an attempt to adjust continually to those realities.

These two subgroups were not in a quest for power merely for selfish interests; they also hoped to shape the new community in ways that would make it more faithful to the divine plan. Significantly, both subgroups (as well as all other biblical models) understand that the divine will includes a relatively equal share in the blessings of the land for all the people. Ezekiel saw that possibility as lying in the direct intervention of Yahweh and the establishment of a new, sacred community which would fulfill God's intentions. The mainline priests saw that possibility as lying in the continued progress of the present (at least presently anticipated) structure so that the normal events of economic life could be adjusted to conform to the divine will. By comparing and contrasting Ezekiel and the priests, the jubilee can be seen, not so much as a utopian concept of another world (even though its regulations may be economically impractical), but as a statement that proper distribution of land can be attained and maintained within the confines of this world.

Part III

THE MORAL WORLD-VIEW OF THE JUBILEE

Chapter 6

THE OBJECTIVE MEANING

The sociology of knowledge has taught us that our understanding of the world—how and why it exists and operates in the ways it does—powerfully affects our behavior. That is to say, our world-view and our moral system are closely related. The land tenure laws of the jubilee display a particular world-view, which in turn underlies a moral system that has implications far beyond mere ownership of the land. Our attempt to discover that world-view will use Mannheim's analysis of the concept of world-view, which was discussed at the end of Chapter 1. It is important to reiterate that the three strata of meaning (objective, expressive and documentary) can be separated only for analytical purposes; they are actually interwoven tightly into a single phenomenon which is the product of the world-view of the actor, whether the actor is aware of it or not. In unravelling these meanings, the world-view of the jubilee will become clear.

In examining the objective meaning, the position of the farmer—for whom the jubilee existed—ought to be recognized. The peasants in the ancient Near East were subsistence farmers who were relatively unin-terested in commercial profit and who always lived at the edge of exis-tence; any economic setback could throw them into a state of permanent dependence.[1] They were interested foremost in *survival*. However, because of factors including climatic variability, imperfect markets and customs, they probably did not maximize their productivity.[2] These small landholders had few liquid reserves—most of their assets con-sisted of the land itself and the few animals they owned which were

1. B. Lang, *Monotheism and the Prophetic Minority: An Essay in Biblical History and Sociology* (The Social World of Biblical Antiquity Series, 1; Sheffield: Almond Press, 1983), p. 117.
2. See M. Lipton, 'The Theory of the Optimizing Peasant', *Journal of Development Studies* (January 1968), pp. 327-32.

considered necessary for survival.[1] If they experienced a bad year, they fell into debt (the collateral for which was their land), but even in good years they were able merely to maintain themselves, not to extricate themselves from the cycle of debt. They were forced to borrow to repay previous debts, and any further difficulties would result in the loss of their land.[2] Thus, the jubilee came into existence in a context where small farms were constantly vulnerable to being absorbed into the large holdings of wealthy creditors, creating a class of landless peasants dependent on the hiring practices of the wealthy for their survival.

Clashing Systems

The jubilee proposes a system that opposed such a route toward debt and the accumulation of land by a small number of people. Indeed, throughout the Hebrew Bible, there is a conflict between competing systems which Brueggemann characterizes in two different ways. First, this clash of systems involves the locus and use of power.[3] On the one hand is the centralized monarchic structure which tends to maintain the status quo and to legitimize the authoritarian rule of the state. Such a power structure benefited the urban classes and the wealthy creditors who were able to accumulate large landholdings and keep the peasants in a dependent status. This system was characteristic of Canaan and was a constant temptation to Israel; David took the first steps toward such a system and Solomon completed the move.[4] On the other hand is the prophetic movement of protest against institutions of power, a movement rooted in the Mosaic tradition of liberation from oppressive monarchy. This movement tended to diffuse power and

1   Neufeld, 'Socio-Economic Background of Yobel', p. 54.

2.   The vulnerability of small farmers can be compared to similar conditions in rural Kenya today as described by P. Collier, 'Malfunctioning of African Rural Factor Markets: Theory and a Kenyan Example', *Oxford Bulletin of Economics and Statistics* 45 (May 1983), pp. 153-55.

3.   W. Brueggemann, 'Trajectories in Old Testament Literature and the Sociology of Ancient Israel', in N.K. Gottwald (ed.), *Bible and Liberation: Political and Social Hermeneutics* (New York: Orbis Books, 1983), pp. 308-15.

4.   See also K. Baltzer, 'Naboths Weinberg (1. Kön. 21): Der Konflict zwischem israelitischem und kanaanäischem Bodenrecht', *Wort und Dienst* 8 (1965), pp. 73-88. The narrative of Ahab's attempt to purchase Naboth's vineyard is a classic example of the clash between the Canaanite system and that represented by the jubilee.

prevent the central authorities from usurping rights and privileges that properly belonged to Yahweh.

The second level of this clash involves the understanding of land itself. In the story of Meribaal's estate (2 Sam. 18-19), land that was once considered a paternal inheritance is transferred to royal ownership, reinforcing the privilege of the monarch to confiscate land and use it as reward or punishment for the subjects.[1] Brueggemann labels this concept of land 'royal/urban', since it rests on the power of the monarchy and benefits the urban class.[2] In this concept of land, possession implies legitimacy, while the landless have no rights, and the king has the power to grant or withdraw possession in accordance with an individual's loyalty.[3] In opposition to such a system was a 'covenantal/ prophetic' model for property ownership which stresses respect for the poor and restraint on the rich.[4] In this model, no one has special privileges of ownership, and land is not understood as a commodity that can be confiscated or purchased, but as a birthright that is inalienable.[5]

If the jubilee represents a system that was in opposition to one which appears to have favored the accumulation of land, what was the actual economic reality within which the jubilee is produced? Morris Silver, an economist, argues that, at least during the eighth and seventh centuries, Israel and Judah enjoyed a vigorous economy from which few, if any, were excluded. He dates the strengthening of their economies at the rise of Omri in the north and Jehoshaphat in the south.[6] At this time, agricultural technology allowed significant increases in productivity, increased diversification (offsetting the risks

1. See Z. Ben-Barak, 'Meribaal and the System of Land Grants in Ancient Israel', *Bib* 62 (1981), pp. 73-91.

2. W. Brueggemann, 'Reflections on Biblical Understandings of Property', *International Review of Mission* 64 (1974), p. 354.

3. On how this compares to the system at Ugarit, see Baltzer, 'Naboths Weinberg', pp. 82-84.

4. Brueggemann, 'Reflections on Biblical Understandings of Property', pp. 354-55.

5. Brueggemann, 'Reflections on Biblical Understandings of Property', p. 356; and H. Schaeffer, *Hebrew Tribal Economy and the Jubilee* (Leipzig: Hinrichs, 1922), p. 73.

6. M. Silver, *Prophets and Markets: The Political Economy of Ancient Israel* (Social Dimensions of Economics; Boston: Kluwer-Nijhoff Publishing, 1983), pp. 1-7.

of blight on a particular crop), and surpluses for export.[1] He acknowledges that with the economic growth and the opening of markets for commodities, there would have followed a consolidation of land which turned small peasant farmers into independent laborers,[2] but this did not affect their real, or even relative, incomes adversely; they merely moved to the cities where 'developments' were built to provide affordable housing.[3] Thus, Silver maintains that income differentials were not very great at this time, and that it was the implementation of the prophetic and Deuteronomic reforms that crippled the economy and led many into poverty.[4]

However, the overwhelming weight of evidence speaks against Silver's thesis. Archaeological excavations have indicated a shift from a rather egalitarian early Israelite society, in which the housing was relatively equal in size and arrangement, to a stratified society during the monarchy, in which there was a considerable difference between the houses of the wealthy and those of the poor.[5] While Silver argues that the references to economic disparity made by the prophets are merely polemical, he does not explain how mere polemics can force the reforms he believes ruined the Israelite economy. If conditions were as favorable as he claims, the burden of proof must lie with his ability to show why a change would have taken place. Gottwald points out that Silver's economic analysis does not consider 'the taxing function of the state and the effects of warfare and political vassalage'.[6] As just noted, David converted patrimonial land into royal land, and that story does not come from the prophetic protest against the monarchy. The increase in the number of landless laborers and the urbanization of the economy tended to disrupt the solidarity of the kinship units which made individuals even more vulnerable to falling into a dependent status.[7] All in all, the prophetic denunciation of latifundism

---

1. Silver, *Prophets and Markets*, pp. 19-24.
2. Silver, *Prophets and Markets*, pp. 259-63.
3. Silver, *Prophets and Markets*, pp. 19, 248.
4. Silver, *Prophets and Markets*, pp. 242, 248.
5. Wenham, *Leviticus*, p. 317. R. de Vaux points specifically to the excavations at Tirsah (modern Tell el-Farah near Nablus) as an example of this shift (*Ancient Israel* [2 vols.; New York: McGraw-Hill, 1965], I, pp. 72-73).
6. Gottwald, *Hebrew Bible*, p. 374 n. 2.
7. G.E. Mendenhall, 'The Hebrew Conquest of Palestine', *BA* 24 (1962), p. 70; and von Waldow, 'Social Responsibility', pp. 196-97.

must be taken at face value.

Even if those peasants who lost their land where able to sell their labor to the large landowners, landless agricultural workers typically earn smaller incomes than landowning peasants.[1] In addition, the landless are much more vulnerable to destitution in periods of crisis than those who farm their own land.[2] With all of this, it appears certain that the peasant farmers were severely hurt under the Canaanite economic system that viewed land as a commodity rather than a birthright. Thus, the jubilee did not present a merely ideological alternative to one particular system, it was a countermeasure to a system that provided wealth for a few at the expense of many. It attempted to restrict the latifundism which was prevalent in the ancient Near East in order to keep the means of production evenly distributed among independent families.[3] Possibly because of that prevalence, the jubilee recognized the constant threat of the loss of land, so it established a means of regaining the proper balance. In addition, it designated the family as the basic landowning entity, ignoring the king altogether, implying that the king had no special privileges in the acquisition of land.

On the other hand, the jubilee also made some compromise with the Canaanite system of land ownership. The Canaanite city-state system and its concept of land ownership existed long before the Israelites took control of Palestine, and some of those cities continued to exist independently until the rise of the monarchy. It would have been virtually impossible to eradicate totally their economic system.[4] Yet when the priests edited the jubilee legislation, they were looking toward the establishment of a new economic order, the old order having been swept away by the Babylonians. Had they chosen to do so, they could have included the cities in the jubilee's provisions. However, since the purpose of the jubilee seems to have been to preserve the economic

---

1. See P. Collier, 'Malfunctioning of African Rural Factor Markets', pp. 153-54.
2. This is dramatically demonstrated by A. Sen, 'Starvation and Exchange Entitlements: A General Approach and its Application to the Great Bengal Famine', *Cambridge Journal of Economics* (January 1977), pp. 46-49, 55.
3. W. Eichrodt, *Theology of the Old Testament*, I, p. 97. Also see R. North, 'The Biblical Jubilee and Social Reform', *Scr* 4 (1951), p. 330.
4. Bess, 'Systems of Land Tenure', pp. 81-82; and Schaeffer, *Hebrew Tribal Economy*, p. 91.

integrity of the peasant farmer, there was no need to protect urban property from alienation.[1] This compromise with the Canaanite system was a concession which was of little importance to the intent of the jubilee.

Land Tenure

The land with which the jubilee was concerned was a specific kind of land. The two words used in Leviticus 25 for a parcel of land are *ăḥuzzâ* and *śādeh.* Gillis Gerleman argues that *'ăḥuzzâ* refers specifically to cultivated land first, because according to Leviticus 27 it is the only land whose worth is capable of being measured by the seed required to sow it, and secondly because it is etymologically related to the concept of 'grasping' which in the case of *'ăḥuzzâ* should be taken in the sense of 'working to produce food'.[2] In support of the latter argument, it should be noted that in the ancient world possession often was determined by whoever cultivated the land,[3] so to work the land was to 'grasp' it as one's own. With regard to *śādeh,* throughout the Holiness Code this word refers only to cultivated land. Therefore, it may be concluded that the jubilee is strictly agrarian legislation whose sole aim is to affect the distribution of land that produces food, that is, land that forms the basis of survival.

Kinship Ownership

But who owned this cultivated land, and how was it owned? Part of understanding the land tenure system assumed by the jubilee is understanding the social consciousness that accompanied it. Neufeld suggests that the prohibition against interest (v. 37) comes from a period of tribal solidarity in which one simply did not exact interest from anyone within the kinship group.[4] This is reinforced by the constant references to 'your brother', which seems to appeal to that sense of

1. Bess, 'Systems of Land Tenure', p. 121.
2. G. Gerleman, 'Nutzrecht und Wohnrecht: Zur Bedeutung von '*ḥzh* und *nḥlh*', *ZAW* 89 (1977), pp. 316-17.
3. Smith, *Religion of the Semites*, p. 96. Cf. P. Collier, 'Malfunctioning of African Rural Factor Markets', p. 158 for an example of a contemporary, pre-industrial society.
4. E. Neufeld, 'Prohibitions against Loans at Interest in Ancient Hebrew Laws', *HUCA* 26 (1955), pp. 407-409.

responsibility toward members of one's own family—'family' meaning the broadest kinship association possible, probably all Israelites. This communal solidarity is also revealed in distaste expressed for allowing a family member to fall into debt slavery and the desire to redeem that person from bondage.[1] It even appears that when one person fell into debt, that individual's family members or even friends might become surety for the loan.[2] The jubilee legislation clearly implies a sense of mutual responsibility that went beyond a modern notion of 'charity'; in effect, it stated, 'we are all in this together, and we all suffer if one of us suffers'.

With such a strong sense of communal solidarity, it might be assumed that land itself was held communally. Indeed, the tradition goes to great lengths to prevent land allotted to a tribe from being alienated from that tribe because of a lack of heirs, for example, provisions for the inheritance rights of daughters, the restriction of their marriages to within the tribe, and levirate marriages. This has led some to conclude that the actual owner of the land was the family, whose interests were protected from an individual's failure, misfortune or whim.[3] K.H. Henrey even claims that the land was owned commonly by the entire tribe, and it was reapportioned periodically by lot.[4] However, the jubilee implies that individual families were alloted particular plots of land from which they could not be alienated (note especially v. 13). In his extensive study, Johannes Pedersen finds 'no evidence of the family having had community of property in the sense that all the members of the family had equal rights of property to a certain piece of ground'.[5] The concepts of tribal solidarity and mutual responsibility would make the relative strength of the tribe as a whole desirable, thus wealth ought to be retained within that broad kinship group. However, it does not necessitate communal ownership of the land.

1. Ginzberg, 'Biblical Economics', pp. 345-51; and Neufeld, 'Socio-Economic Background of Yobel', p. 98.

2. Neufeld, 'Socio-Economic Background of Yobel', pp. 78-81.

3. See North, 'The Biblical Jubilee', p. 332; *Sociology of the Biblical Jubilee*, p. 175.

4. K.H. Henrey, 'Land Tenure in the Old Testament', *PEQ* 86 (1954), pp. 5-15.

5. J. Pedersen, *Israel: Its Life and Culture* (2 vols.; London: Oxford University Press, 1926), I, p. 85.

Israel is not alone as a preindustrial society to have a land tenure system that mixes individual and kinship rights. On Rarotonga—the largest of the Cook Islands—land was divided among the several descent groups, with a strong bond between the particular kinship groups and their land, which was 'subject to interests and rights of more than one person'.[1] The Inca empire had an elaborate system of communal tenure in which each man was allotted land according to the size and composition of his family. At times a family plot could be bequeathed to a son, but it was not transferable in any other way.[2] In his study of land tenure in preindustrial societies, R.W.G. Bryant finds several common elements.[3] First, religion (often ancestor worship) plays an important role in the control of the land displaying itself in patriarchal or feudal control. Secondly, the one who actually cultivates the land retains the right of usufruct of that land. Thirdly, social responsibilities are woven into the rights to property in such a way that the absolute ownership of land is invested with the tribe, individuals holding certain plots by mutual consent and subject to custom. Finally, land is not subject to being bought or sold without consultation with other family members.

Asiatic Mode of Production
It has been suggested that the land tenure system proposed by the jubilee might best be understood as an example of the Asiatic mode of production (hereafter, AMP). In order to evaluate that thesis, it will be necessary to examine the AMP itself, which has very deep roots. Aristotle believed that in an Asiatic despotism, the population was a 'community of slaves' that had no rights under a sovereign who enjoyed general legitimacy.[4] In the fourteenth century, after Aristotle had been translated into Latin, Asiatic despotism became linked with the absence of private property.[5] During the sixteenth and early

1. R.W.G. Bryant, *Land: Private Property, Public Control* (Montreal: Harvest House, 1972), pp. 18-19.
2. Bryant, *Land*, pp. 26-27. In various regions of rural Kenya, between three and nineteen per cent of the land was purchased or being rented—the rest had been inherited. Collier, 'Malfunctioning of African Rural Factor Markets', p. 156.
3. Bryant, *Land*, pp. 22-23.
4. M. Sawer, *Marxism and the Question of the Asiatic Mode of Production* (The Hague: Martinus Nijhoff, 1977), p. 5.
5. Sawer, *Marxism and the Question of the Asiatic Mode of Production*, p. 6.

seventeenth centuries, political writers such as Machiavelli, Bodin, Bacon and Hobbes compared the Turkish and Muscovite empires with the European monarchies and concluded that, in the Asian empires, the ruler retained possession of the land, goods and people of the country.[1] Seventeenth-century travellers to Persia and Mogul India concluded that the emperor was the sole owner of all the land, but there was debate on whether the ownership caused his power or his power caused the ownership.[2] John Stuart Mill believed that the oriental economy was able to progress to sedentary agriculture because of the irrigation systems built, maintained and administered by the state; therefore, the state owned the land, but the peasants retained the usufruct.[3]

Of course, the one who brought the notion of the AMP into the modern world was Karl Marx.[4] During the nineteenth century more attention was focused on the village community in India with the assumption that they represented an early stage of development in Indo-European socio-economic life. Out of this grew the controversy of the existence of primitive agrarian communism. Even though Marx never achieved a systematic theory, he used the AMP in his ideological critique of the capitalist mode of production. Marx postulated that early clans produced the means of survival communally. As larger groups formed, the land continued to be owned by the 'unity' personified in a leader or a god while the individual families or villages were the hereditary proprietors. Marx's ethnological research (mistaken as it was) led him to conclude that land in India could not be alienated without the consent of the village community. Where the climatic conditions required major public works for the development and maintenance of irrigation systems, there was a further central-

---

1. A. Bailey and J. Llobera, 'The Asiatic Mode of Production: Sources and Formation of the Concept', in A. Bailey and J. Llobera, *The Asiatic Mode of Production: Science and Politics* (London: Routledge & Kegan Paul, 1981), pp. 16-17. Sawer points out that some of these writers saw Asiatic despotism as a positive counter-example to the abuse of feudal privilege that was rampant in Europe (*Marxism and the Asiatic Mode of Production*, p. 9).

2. Bailey and Llobera, 'The Asiatic Mode of Production', p. 18; and Sawer, *Marxism and the Asiatic Mode of Production*, pp. 9-12.

3. Bailey and Llobera, 'The Asiatic Mode of Production', p. 21.

4   For this analysis of Marx's understanding of the AMP, see Bailey and Llobera, 'The Asiatic Mode of Production' pp. 22-36; and Sawer, *Marxism and the Asiatic Mode of Production*, pp. 43-44.

ization of power and the development of the state, which, once in existence, acted in the interest of the ruling class. In the end, the AMP could be just as oppressive as any system of private ownership.

It is Gottwald who has used the AMP to aid our understanding of the foundations of Israel's land tenure system.[1] First, Gottwald suggests that the Canaanite system must be distinguished from European feudalism because (1) Canaan lacked any tenurial or personal relations between the rulers and the ruled and (2) Canaan was experiencing a rise in state authority and trade. Secondly, he claims that there was a significant amount of hydraulic activity within Syro-Palestine and a tremendous influence from the great 'river civilizations' to replicate their political organization. From this he concludes that the village tribalism of early Israel was actually imposed upon them by the central authorities as might be predicted by the model of the AMP. When the peasants revolted and formed the Israelite tribal confederation, the village community persisted because there was no real private ownership of the means of production; thus, private capital was not accumulated in a few hands, and the villages were not destroyed by unattached labor. What the Israelites did was to transfer the ultimate ownership of their land from the central authorities of the Canaanite city-states to Yahweh, the God who liberated them.

Individual Family Ownership

The jubilee's insistence that Yahweh is the owner of all the land and that the people are his slaves who are tenants on the land certainly suggests a tenure system resembling the AMP. However, one very important element in the jubilee legislation that alters this perception is the *gô'ēl*. The existence of a system of redemption implies that land can be sold to another citizen, something that would be impossible under the AMP since the state owns all the land in the first place. Thus, the jubilee presupposes the existence of independent entities within society that have the right to buy and sell land, and it does not attempt to abrogate that right. The purpose of the *gô'ēl* is not to prevent such sales, but to rectify the imbalance produced by the sale. Many scholars have argued that the restoration of a proper balance

1. This analysis is found in N.K. Gottwald, 'Early Israel and "The Asiatic Mode of Production" in Canaan', in *SBL Seminar Papers* (Missoula, MT: Scholars Press, 1976), pp. 145-54.

meant the retention of the land within the tribe or clan.[1] For them, the one whose incompetence or misfortune led to the loss of the land did not regain that land unless he himself redeemed it; if a family member redeemed the land, that person kept it. The proper balance was maintained because the land remained within the kinship group which is assumed to be the actual owner of the land. The function of the jubilee was to restore the land to the kinship group in the event of there being no redeemer within the family.

However, the jubilee legislation treats the process of redemption as an alternative to waiting until the year of the jubilee, an alternative which accomplishes the same end. Verses 25-28 appear to list three ways in which an individual who has lost his land through poverty might regain that land: (1) a family member may redeem it, (2) he may redeem it himself, or, if those two alternatives are impossible, (3) the land will be returned in the jubilee. (The same alternatives are provided with regard to the sale of a person to a foreigner [vv. 47-54].) It is clear that during the jubilee the land returns to the original holder, not to the kinship group in general, and if the individual redeems the land, it obviously reverts to him. There are no distinctions made among these alternatives; therefore, it seems that the *gô'ēl* is obligated to buy the land out of a sense of communal responsibility, not because the land is owned communally.

Bryant's land tenure studies of preindustrial societies concluded that the right to a land's usufruct entailed social responsibilities, and that applies to a broad notion of communal solidarity present in the jubilee, but in the legislation as it now exists, the kinship group does not exert ownership rights. What the kinship group retains is the responsibility to protect the rights of the members of the family from losing their land. As is also shown by the curse placed on those who move boundary markers (Deut. 19.14; 27.15; and Hos. 5.10), private holdings of particular plots of land were carefully guarded, belying a primitive communism.[2] On the other hand, the land tenure system

1.   See R. Westbrook, 'Redemption of Land', *Israel Law Review* 6 (1971), pp. 369-70; Bess, 'Land Tenure', p. 80; Neufeld, 'The Socio-Economic Background of Yobel', pp. 74-77; Pedersen, *Israel*, I, p. 84; Schaeffer, *Hebrew Tribal Economy*, p. 71; and de Vaux, *Ancient Israel*, I, p. 167.

2.   See F. Horst, 'Das Eigentum nach dem Alten Testament', in *Gottes Recht* (Munich: Chr. Kaiser Verlag, 1961), p. 211; and North, *Sociology of the Biblical Jubilee*, pp. 161-65.

implied by the jubilee cannot be understood as 'private ownership' in the modern, Western sense. An individual (family) had a right to occupy and farm a particular plot of land and, on the surface, the right to buy and sell land. However, the jubilee states quite clearly that such 'sales' cannot be permanent; thus an individual does not have an absolute right of disposal over the land. Verse 16 indicates that any transaction is in reality a leasing of the usufruct rights of the land.

The jubilee does deal with individual rights; it does not so subordinate the individual to the community as to sacrifice the welfare of the individual for the good of the group. The redeemer is not merely retaining tribal wealth within the tribe, but is restoring a person to the land. In addition, the jubilee is dealing with a particular kind of land, land that is used to grow food and provide the essentials for survival. Such land has a special character in that it is not subject to the economic rules that govern normal transactions; such land is not a commodity, and even the one who has a right to use it does not have the right to sell it. The jubilee recognizes certain contingencies which may necessitate the need for liquid assets; thus there is the provision for 'leasing' the land, but there are strict limitations placed on that provision so that a particular family is permanently granted the rights to a particular piece of arable land. In an agrarian society, that is seen as a guarantee of economic security.[1] The periodic 'reform' which characterizes the jubilee adds to our understanding of its objective meaning.

Land Reform

North sees the sabbath-year law as an integral part of the process of the jubilee. North assumes that the 'leasing' of the usufruct rights was actually a method of repaying a debt, the produce of the land being a payment against the interest and principle. In the seventh year, the debtor-farmer was allowed the produce from the land by which (if he were able) he could pay off his debts and be free. In the event of the allowance not being sufficient to clear the debt, the usufruct rights returned to the creditor for another six years. If the debt had not been repaid after seven such cycles, it was simply cancelled, and the debtor

---

1. Collier points out that conditions restricting land transactions can actually work to the detriment of the smallest landholders ('Malfunctioning of African Rural Factor Markets', pp. 158-59). However, the jubilee presupposes an equal allotment and is not intended to be literal legislation anyway.

earned 'retirement' from his service.[1] However, interesting though this thesis may be, the text does not support it. The sabbath year is strictly a year of rest for the land; it is not to be worked by anyone. Whether one may eat the spontaneous produce of the land is unclear, but there is no connection to debt or debt repayment. All laws dealing with the maintenance of a proper distribution of land are associated with the jubilee year.

Regarding the jubilee, North theorizes that it was only intended as a unique event.

> The legislator intended the 50-year respite for *once*: a single fresh start for the bankrupt Israelite. He does not exclude the desirability of its repetition at fifty year intervals forever after... But to decree this so far in advance would merit the reproach of academic theorizing.[2]

He also claims that the phrase 'the land shall not be sold in perpetuity' of v. 23 refers only to the initial fifty-year period following the allotment of the land by Joshua.[3] However, the casuistic parts of the early sections of the legislation (vv. 14, 25-31, 35-36, 39-40, 47-48, 53) bear the marks of simple law intended to be obeyed indefinitely. When the priests incorporated the older law into their own code, they added the cultic interpretations (vv. 8-12) which imply the sense of a recurring ritual, not a one-time event. The text of the jubilee legislation ought to be taken as a proposal for an ongoing system of land redistribution.

North goes on to assert that following the initial fifty-year period, the jubilee was a limit to the number of years a debtor had to work for a creditor (as described above). In this case, the jubilee was particular for each case; therefore, there was not an economic upheaval every fifty years when all debts in the nation were cancelled at one time. North argues that the phrases in the text that seem to make the jubilee universal are 'relatively few', and the jubilee is related to slave-release laws which were particular (cf. Exod. 21.1-6).[4] If the jubilee was an attempt to produce civic law that was to be obeyed literally and could be coordinated with other existing slave and debt laws in the Covenant and Deuteronomic Codes, North's hypothesis

1. North, 'The Biblical Jubilee', pp. 333-34; *Sociology of the Biblical Jubilee*, pp. 156-57, 186-87.
2. North, *Sociology of the Biblical Jubilee*, pp. 207-208.
3. North, *Sociology of the Biblical Jubilee*, p. 209.
4. North, *Sociology of the Biblical Jubilee*, p. 174.

would deserve serious consideration. However, those 'relatively few' phrases do exist, and the jubilee is an independent entity with its own meaning. One cannot escape the conclusion that, objectively, the jubilee proposed a periodic (every fifty years) land distribution that would restore every individual family to the land to which it had an absolute right. Objectively, that sort of radical periodic reform would have been very difficult to administer and might have been economically disastrous;[1] therefore, we need to move to the expressive meaning of the jubilee to understand its intent.

---

1.   See N.M. Soss, 'Old Testament Law and Economic Society', *Journal of the History of Ideas*, 34 (1973), pp. 323-44.

Chapter 7

THE EXPRESSIVE MEANING

Clues from the Social Location of the Priests

We have already examined the place and function which the priests filled during the exile when they adopted the jubilee into their own legal code; now we must determine what this tells us about the expressive meaning of the jubilee. Kenelm Burridge distinguishes between 'cults' and 'movements' by suggesting that a cult is firmly organized and static, being concerned with a particular source of power, whereas a movement attempts to spread its ideas and organization more widely.[1] The priests displayed characteristics of both; they had a clear organization and an exclusive membership, yet they held an ideology which they hoped to impose on the whole people. The jubilee must be seen as part of the drive of the priests to revitalize the nation during the period of crisis. Anthony Wallace describes six forms of revitalization movements; nativistic, which eliminates the alien; revivalistic, which recaptures the tradition; cargo cults, which import the alien through ships; vitalistic, which introduces new things; millenarian, which is apocalyptic; and messianic, which relies on a divine savior. These forms can be subsumed under three ideal types—revivals, importations and utopias.[2]

The characteristics displayed by the priests seem to conform most closely with the revivalistic type. The very nature of the priesthood focused on traditions that were safeguarded by this group of elite bearers of esoteric knowledge. The traditional knowledge was not secret knowledge, but the priests had a vested interest in claiming

---

1. K. Burridge, *New Heaven, New Earth: A Study of Millenarian Activities* (New York: Schocken Books, 1969), p. 12 n. 1.
2. A.F.C. Wallace, 'Revitalization Movements', *American Anthropologist* 58 (1965), pp. 267-75.

authority for the traditions since without them the priesthood could not exist. Thus, the jubilee was a part of a revivalistic movement in which the old traditions were being reclaimed and proclaimed as vital for the survival of the Yahwistic community. It is true that this particular priesthood was located in a special situation as the locus of authority for a group of exiles who were hoping to return to their home and (re-)establish their nation, but this is not utopianism. While the priests, through their legal code, were establishing the constitution of a truly Yahwistic community that would conform to their ideal—as opposed to the reality of the exile, or even the monarchy—the jubilee looks to the past for its structure. The ancestors had the right ideals, but they never carried them out; to fulfill those traditional ideals would be to revive the real Yahwistic community.

Does the social location of the priests express anything about the nature of that community? There are those who believe the jubilee actually bestowed power on the priests through its control of land distribution. By this hypothesis, the very fact that the priests were codifying the law and that the law included the provisions found in the jubilee meant that the jubilee granted the priests the power to distribute the land to themselves or their supporters, giving them virtual control of the agrarian economy. However, the jubilee worked automatically, independent from priestly prerogatives, and it tended to maintain a relatively equal distribution of the land, dispersing economic power widely. At most, the priests may have wanted to establish the returning exiles' right to their 'fair share' of the land; however, had they wanted control of the distribution of the land, they could have stated that explicitly in the legislation; the simple presence of the jubilee in the Priestly Code does not express a grab for power by the priests.

If the priests were not expressing a desire for power through the jubilee, perhaps they were expressing a desire for national security. Taking the role of legislators and leaders of the new community, perhaps they also believed it was their duty to provide for the military defense of the people. M. Weber argues:

> Wherever military power rested on self-equipment of free landowners, land ownership was a function of military qualification. Similarly, the desire to preserve the 'name' of the sib in Israel, which was decisive for the levirate and related institutions, had in addition to religious probably also military foundations.[1]

1.   M. Weber, *Ancient Judaism* (trans. and ed. H.H. Gerth and D. Martindale;

The maintenance of a broadly based civilian militia would require that the civilian population had the economic means to provide its own weaponry. Of course, no civilian militia would possess sophisticated or expensive equipment, but even a good sword or spear would require funds not needed for the survival of the family. Weber's hypothesis might apply to the premonarchic period when Israel relied upon such a militia, but David introduced the use of a professional army, and Israel depended on paid soldiers during the rest of its existence so any provision for the self-equipment of a civilian militia would have been unnecessary. The priests' projection of a restored community, on the other hand, appeared to take into consideration the reality of ancient Near East imperialism. The new nation would be a Yahwistic community existing under the hegemony of the Persians; thus, the priests were leaders of the religious and social life of the community, but the Persians would deal with military matters. The jubilee as we now have it was not an attempt to give a sword to every family.

The social location of the priests, as well as the rest of their writings, does tend to suggest that the jubilee was an expression of the need for order. Throughout the ancient Near East, offenses against justice for the weak were considered offenses against the cosmic order.[1] For any society to survive, it must act in harmony with the cosmic order or it risks the suicide of falling into chaos. Therefore, the religious leaders of the ancient Near Eastern cultures admonished the nations' leaders and citizens to practice the kind of righteousness that upheld good order and ensured the survival of the cosmos.[2] For the priests, the jubilee was another means whereby the proper cosmic order could be upheld and the world could be protected from chaos. The offenses of the pre-exilic period undermined the order of the universe, and the result was the destruction of Israel and the threat of the disintegration of Yahwism itself, and the jubilee was intended to prevent the same abuses of the wealthy against the poor that led to such an imbalance.

New York: The Free Press, 1967), p. 73.

1.   H.H. Schmid, *Gerechtigkeit als Weltordnung* (Tübingen: Mohr [Paul Siebeck], 1968), p. 85.

2.   For a complete study of this issue, see Schmid's work and D. Knight, 'Cosmogonic Traditions and Ethical Order', in R. Lovin and F. Reynolds (eds.), *Cosmogony and Ethical Order: New Studies in Comparative Ethics* (Chicago: University of Chicago Press, 1985), pp. 133-57.

But that is a very general statement of intent; the expressive meaning of the jubilee must be examined in more detail.

Clues from the Other Jubilee Laws

The legislation on the land was set in the context of a greater complex of laws, and an examination of those laws will help in understanding the intent of land tenure regulations. The issue of the fallow years was complicated by the presence of contradictory statements coming from different levels of tradition. The original fallow law of 25.3-5 prohibited any gathering of food which led to the addition of vv. 20-22 that explained how the people are to survive a fallow period. However, priestly editors amended the sabbath law to indicate that the 'sabbath of the land' was to become food for the people, particularly the disenfranchised and even the beasts (vv. 6-7). Remarkably, in v. 11 one of the editors repeated the absolute prohibition of food gathering found in the original law and then declared that the people may eat of the produce of the field (*śādeh*) in v. 12. Porter attempts to reconcile these statements by claiming that, during the fallow year, one could not eat anything that grew in cultivated land—the indirect result of human · labor—but food that grew wild could be consumed.[1] However, *śādeh* also refers to cultivated land; therefore, this solution seems inadequate. Verses 11-12 form the link between the jubilee legislation and the sabbath in that they parallel vv. 4-8. The priests were more concerned with literary connectedness than with literal internal consistency. If exact compliance with particular fallow laws had been the priests' aim, they could have increased the clarity of the regulations instead of adding to the confusion; however, it seems they were more interested in declaring the sanctity of the year and the implications for sharing with the poor (vv. 6a-7). The very confusion of the fallow laws may indicate that the priests were operating at a level deeper than blind obedience to detailed legislation.

Another important section of the jubilee legislation dealt with slavery. This material was complicated as well, but because of various categories of slavery, not because of internal contradictions. The first category involved the slavery of an impoverished Israelite to another Israelite. North claims that this relationship was the same as that granted to an alien refugee by Yahweh, that is, one of protection and

---

1.   Porter, *Leviticus*, pp. 198-99.

support by the master and loyal service by the slave.[1] However, within this category, it appears that the one who sold himself into debt bondage remains in service until the jubilee, which explains the absence of any discussion concerning redemption in vv. 39-43.[2] The priests added the comment that this relationship is not true slavery because the Israelites were actually God's slaves and cannot be owned by anyone else. The priests also added the second category of slavery, the slavery of foreigners to an Israelite. Because foreigners were not God's slaves, they could be owned, sold and bequeathed as any other property. The third category involves the slavery of an Israelite to a foreigner, in which case, a relative was to redeem the individual as quickly as possible. Apparently the fraternal bond among Israelites was to ensure the proper treatment of fellow Israelite servants; however, the sale of an Israelite to a foreigner meant the possibility of permanent slavery, and that individual must be rescued from such a threat. In spite of the obvious double standard, the legislation was intended to prevent Israelites from falling into a situation of permanent subservience and utter dependence.

What linked all the jubilee laws was the issue of debt and interest-taking; they all dealt with situations which arise when an individual fell into debt and the creditor sought repayment. The legislation recognized that situations arise in which one person must borrow money or food from another in order to survive and that to prohibit *debt* would destroy the poor. However, these regulations put strict limits on the administration of debt, restricting the power of the creditor to take permanent possession of pledges given for a loan— whether that pledge was a person or property. Verse 36 even prohibited the exaction of interest on loans to persons who had been reduced to poverty. North argues that some interest was allowed on loans in order to give some incentive to moneylenders to take the risk of lending to the poor.[3] Because laws are responses to existing situations and not hypothetical ones, it is undoubtedly true that the poor were being charged interest on loans. However, the ancient admonition must be taken seriously; the sustaining of the poverty-stricken was not to be a profit-making enterprise. The old law even used two words for interest— *nešek* and *t/marbît*. By examining the

1.   North, 'The Biblical Jubilee and Social Reform', p. 325.
2.   Horst, 'Das Eigentum nach dem Alten Testament', p. 219.
3.   North, *Sociology of the Biblical Jubilee*, pp. 178-79.

roots of the words, some have concluded that *nešek* ('bite') refers to interest deducted from the loan before it is given, while *t/marbît* ('increase') refers to interest added to the repayment.[1] Verse 37 suggests that *nešek* refers to interest on loans of money, while *t/marbît* refers to interest on loans of food.[2] The first interpretation implies an *inclusio* which encompasses all conceivable types of interest, whereas the second deals with loans often needed by the poor. Perhaps both interpretations ought to be kept in mind as we examine this issue.

Many older scholars assume the prohibition against interest-taking stems from a period when Israel's economy was too primitive to make use of commercial loans; therefore, all loans were designed for helping the poor.[3] However, as stated above, these laws responded to an existing situation; thus the prohibition against interest presupposes the common use of interest in giving loans, not a primitive economy.[4] The tradition which the priests took up and passed on was a prohibition stated in the context of extending credit to poverty-stricken Israelites. Particularly by the time the priests edited the jubilee legislation, commercial loans were commonplace; therefore, the expressive meaning of this law ought not to be taken as a blanket prohibition on all loans but a provision to protect the poor from moneylenders attempting to profit from their pain.

Bernhard Lang suggests that there were three alternative relationships between the rich and the poor—'patronage', which involved mutual responsibility, 'partnership' which involved mutual investment or 'exploitation' in which the creditor's sole interest was in making a profit.[5] These laws, as well as comments by the prophets and the sages, indicate that the peasants were being exploited by the upper class, and this maltreatment was considered an injustice not to be tolerated

1. H. Gamoren, 'The Biblical Law against Loans on Interest', *JNES* 30, p. 131; Neufeld 'Prohibitions against Loans', pp. 355-57.
2. S.E. Loewenstamm, '*m/trbyt* and *nšk*', *JBL* 88 (1969), pp. 78-80; Noth, *Leviticus*, p. 191.
3. Neufeld, 'Prohibitions against Loans', pp. 339-60. For example, see Gamoren, 'The Biblical Law against Loans on Interest', who sees part of the reason for the uniqueness of this law in its beginnings in the pastoral context of the desert, where there was no need for commercial loans.
4. Westbrook, 'Jubilee Laws', p. 212.
5. Lang, *Monotheism and the Prophetic Minority*, pp. 118-19.

within the Yahwistic community. Debt appears to have been considered a necessary evil which, if administered properly, could mean survival for a poor family but, if allowed to be a profitable business, could mean perpetual dependence and destitution. Thus, these jubilee laws on interest expressed the desire to break the cycle of debt and dependence in which the poor found themselves. As Sharon Ringe points out:

> Like the laws concerning the release of slaves, provisions for a return to one's land imply the cancellation of debts. With the restoration of real estate, however, the former debtor could hope to attain economic independence instead of merely beginning a new cycle of poverty and indebtedness.[1]

The land could be used as a pledge for a loan to help the poor through particularly difficult periods, but it was also a barrier against grinding debt and the threat of exploitation by greedy moneylenders, and it was a means to self-reliance.

Clues from the Form

As Mannheim points out, the form of a social phenomenon (in this case a document) is an excellent indicator of its expressive meaning.[2] The most obvious aspect of the form of Leviticus 25 is the fact that it was presented as legal material. Here the issue of land tenure was not handled through historical narrative, as in Joshua 13–19, or prophetic utterance, as in Ezekiel 47–48, but through civil laws given theological warrants. In general, law serves a society by bearing its notions of what is sacred, just and right, and it provides not only specific rules to guard those notions but also a coherent system of principles that forms the framework of an orderly world.[3] Undoubtedly, those who promulgate law also have motives of self-interest, so the law can become a device for furthering certain goals; however, even selfish interests are a part of a larger world-view which is embodied within the law. The priests subsumed all relations between God and the world under their legal code, 'which brought about the subordination of all existing things to the sovereign governing will of the transcendent God'.[4] Thus, the articulation of the jubilee concept in legal terms indicates that it was understood to be an integral and permanent part

---

1. Ringe, *Jesus, Liberation, and the Biblical Jubilee*, p. 27.
2. Mannheim, 'Interpretation of *Weltanschauung*', p. 52.
3. D. Patrick, *Old Testament Law* (Atlanta: John Knox, 1985), pp. 1-4.
4. Eichrodt, *Theology of the Old Testament*, II, p. 174.

of the divinely ordained cosmic structure, not a unique aberration from the norm enacted by human agents.

James Leovy and Greer Taylor have suggested an analysis of the stages of legal development which may provide further insight into the nature of the jubilee.[1] Legal systems grow out of social experience and only as experience elicits a need, and they then develop in stages according to the changing needs of the community. The first stage is the 'strict law' stage which occurs at a society's early formation when the consequences of potentially divisive events must be limited. These laws tend to be casuistic, self-identifying, self-applying and self-evident. The second stage is the 'stage of equity' in which the interests of weaker groups in society are protected for the sake of a more unified society in face of external threats. It tends toward the pole of freedom and equity rather than security and stability, and it is apodictic law based on moral principles. The third stage is 'codification' in which the self-evident principles of the stage of equity are more clearly defined through some legislative process (real or fictional) and applied through a juridical process. The fourth stage follows a serious upheaval when basic tenets of right and wrong must be established and is generally a return to strict law. The individual forms a contract to obey the law precisely for the good of the society.

One can see some of these stages in the development of the jubilee. The first stratum of Leviticus 25, a 'debt-sale law',[2] displays the language of neutral casuistic law (the characteristic *'îšî* followed by *wĕ'im*). While that form would indicate Leovy and Taylor's first stage of legal development, the content tends toward the second, the attempt to protect the weaker members of the society. The second stratum, a redaction which adds the term 'jubilee',[3] takes the jubilee law completely into the second stage. Patrick distinguishes between casuistic remedial law, which is impersonal and provides the remedy in the apodosis to the problem in the protasis, and casuistic primary law, which tends toward the second person and provides rights and privileges to particular relationships.[4] This redaction introduced the second person into the jubilee laws and began the addition of theological

---

1. J.G. Leovy and G.M. Taylor, 'Law and Social Development in Israel,' *ATR* 39 (1957), pp. 14-23.
2. See Fager, 'Land Tenure and the Biblical Jubilee', pp. 92-97.
3. Fager, 'Land Tenure and the Biblical Jubilee', pp. 92-97.
4. Patrick, *Old Testament Law*, pp. 23-24.

warrants for legislation. By that time, the regulations dealing with equitable land tenure were moving in the direction of principles rather than narrow rules although they were still expressed as individual laws. It is difficult to determine when the jubilee attained Leovy and Taylor's third stage—codification. Depending on how narrowly one defines 'code', either RJub codified the jubilee into the Holiness Code or the priests did so in their code.

If the priests were the first to codify the jubilee, it would appear to be a codification at the fourth stage of legal development. However, it would be misleading to say simply that this was a return to the strict law stage; the other stages had occurred and their marks remained in the jubilee legislation. The priests retained the second person form and added to the theological warrants, and the content remained focused on the protection of the weak. It is certainly the case that the Priestly Code followed a serious upheaval, and the basic tenets of social life had to be re-established and enforced. The priests seemed to want absolute compliance with their law in order to maintain the new social order that was about to be born, but a distinction must be made between moral law, which is governed by social mores, and judicial law, which can be and is enforced by the use of sanctions.[1] The jubilee legislation is devoid of sanctions, and thus obedience must be elicited by appeal to the theological and moral sensibilities of the community.

This appeal is expressed most strongly in the so-called 'motive clauses'. As one might suspect from Leovy and Taylor's study, the incidence of motive clauses increases over the development of the legal codes even though the clauses themselves appear to be quite ancient.[2] Although motive clauses occur elsewhere in ancient Near Eastern literature, only in the Hebrew Bible are they formulated in the second person and do they introduce extrinsic motivations rather than merely underlining a key element within the law itself.[3] While B. Gemser believes the motive clause 'I am the Lord your God' has its setting in cultic recitation,[4] Rifat Sonsino recognizes a similarity

---

1. Patrick, *Old Testament Law*, pp. 5-6.
2. B. Gemser, 'Motive Clauses in Old Testament Law' (VTSup, 1; Leiden: Brill 1953), pp. 51-52; and R. Sonsino, *Motive Clauses in Hebrew Law: Biblical Forms and Near Eastern Parallels* (SBLDS, 45; Chico, CA: Scholars Press, 1980), pp. 225-26.
3. Sonsino, *Motive Clauses in Hebrew Law*, p. 224.
4. Gemser, 'Motive Clauses in Old Testament Law', p. 63.

between motive clauses in wisdom and those in the law. He concludes that 'a teaching function...rather than an alleged cultic preaching seems to be reflected best in the use of the legal motive clauses.[1] More specifically, his analysis of the conditional forms of the law found in Leviticus 25 indicates that their original setting was in the instructions of those in authority.[2] It seems the priests' intent was to reinforce the theological warrant behind the law and the impact of the personal relationship between Yahweh and the people of Israel.[3]

This theological grounding of the jubilee legislation was expressed not only by the motive clauses, but also by the fact of its becoming cultic legislation. RJub had already introduced the blowing of the horn on the fiftieth year (vv. 8-9a), but the priests clearly defined the year of jubilee as 'sanctified' (vv. 9b-12). The provisions of the jubilee are not merely civil regulations carried out in the normal process of human government, but they are carried out within the confines of sacred time as an act of religious righteousness before God. The cultic nature of the jubilee expresses the notion that proper ownership by God entails acts which benefit the poor.[4] The implementation of the belief in an equitable distribution of the land is a sacred act defined by proper rituals and times that express its holiness. The fact that the priests turned the jubilee into cultic law reinforced by the motive clause 'I am the Lord your God' removed the issue of land tenure from the realm of economic expediency and introduced it into that of divine interest. The priests intended to make the issue of land tenure one of cosmic importance, the neglect of which would court a return to chaos.

The priests set all of this law in the context of Mount Sinai and Mosaic proclamations (vv. 1-2). One may assume from this that the priests looked upon Moses as one who carried sufficient authority to elicit obedience to the laws. Thus, the priests turned to a 'semi-legendary' figure of the remote past to be the source of the social structure of the new community to be built after the exile. Regarding the sabbath years in particular, the priests recognized that the forebears had not obeyed the law (Lev. 26.34-35). Their ancestors had the proper law (Moses had given it to them) to create a just and righteous society, but

1. Sonsino, *Motive Clauses in Hebrew Law*, p. 225.
2. Sonsino, *Motive Clauses in Hebrew Law*, pp. 219-21.
3. Patrick, *Old Testament Law*, p. 154.
4. North, *Sociology of the Biblical Jubilee*, pp. 219-21.

they had failed to do so, and the penalty had been the exile. The old ideals were fine; what the new community must do is actually execute the ancient values. The jubilee was expressed as a message from the past—one that had been forgotten, but one that society had been carrying with it throughout the generations. The advantage of this approach was its appeal to the familiar and the stable; by placing the jubilee within the context of Mosaic law, the priests reinforced the notion of a stable cosmos in which the people could survive if they were obedient to the cosmic order.

The priests also introduced the past by alluding to the liberation of the people from Egypt and the conquest of the land of Canaan (vv. 38, 42, 55). These historical allusions expressed three beliefs. First, they claimed the people as the exclusive possession of Yahweh, who was the subject of the acts of liberation and conquest, therefore legitimating the deity's right to regulate the social life of the community. (This will be explored in more detail below.) Secondly, any oppression of the poor was seen as a repudiation of Yahweh's liberating act in the exodus.[1] If Yahweh chose these former slaves to be free, any attempt to return them to a state of subservience would deny God's sovereign will. Finally, the historical allusions expressed the belief that the land was a gift from God, unearned by the people either through their effort or their merit. The subtle reference to God's bringing the people to the land of Canaan was a reminder that the land did not 'naturally' belong to the people, that is, it was not in the cosmic order of things that *this* people owned *this* land.[2] If the people had no natural right to the land, they had no absolute right of disposal over it, and Yahweh's original intent in giving the land had to be honored.

Clues from the Concept of Divine Ownership

If the existence of the jubilee and the sabbath implied Yahweh's ownership of the land, the priests stated it explicitly in v. 23. In addition, v. 55 declared that Yahweh owned the people of Israel as well as their land. Indeed, the concept of divine ownership of land and people appears to occupy a foundational position in the jubilee legislation as the priests handed it on to us. All of the laws concerning the sale of land and persons rested on the belief that Yahweh, as ultimate owner

---

1.   Von Waldow, 'Social Responsibility', pp. 200-202.
2.   See Wildberger, 'Israel und sein Land', p. 409.

of both, had privilege of sovereignty that could not be abrogated. God was portrayed as 'the liege lord' who owned the land and its produce and the people and their service.[1] The priests also expressed the relationship between Yahweh and Israel as one of patron and client—the Israelites were 'sojourners' with God. Either as slaves or foreign clients, the people of Israel were portrayed as subordinate and subservient to Yahweh—a people whose ultimate and absolute loyalty belonged to the deity and not to any human master.[2] To put themselves or their land at the absolute disposal of anyone other than Yahweh would have been an act of disloyalty, a denial of the owner's rights.

In addition to being an expression of total subservience, the concept of divine ownership or patronage spoke of dependence. It seems that before the exile *gērîm* were characteristically landless, which may be reflected in the juxtaposition of the declarations that Yahweh was the owner of the land and that the people were God's *gērîm*.[3] To be landless in an agrarian society was to be dependent on another to provide the means of survival. Generally, this meant the need to have a wealthy person pay for one's labor with food, money or the right to work a small plot of land. The analogy of wage labor ought not to be pushed very far, but it could be construed that Yahweh was granting Israel the means of survival (land and the blessings of the land) in exchange for their loyal service. There was a greater sense of 'giftedness' than this in the jubilee. However, it is clear that the people were to remember that they were not able to survive by their own efforts, rather it was by the grace of God that they had land at all and that the land produced food. The people were dependent on the owner of the land for their life.

When these expressions of dependence and subservience are combined with the belief that Yahweh is a god of justice, the concept of divine ownership of the land reinforced the demand for justice among the people. The jubilee rested upon the assumption that all Israelites were attached to family land allotted to the several families at the time of the conquest of Canaan; therefore there was the basic presupposition that God willed all Israelites to have a relatively equal opportunity to

1. A. van Selms, *Year of Jubilee* (IDBSup; Nashville: Abingdon Press, 1962), p. 498; and Wildberger, 'Israel und sein Land', pp. 411-12.
2. Wildberger, 'Israel und sein Land', p. 418.
3. Weber, *Ancient Judaism*, pp. 33, 71.

share in the richness of the land. The jubilee then became a mechanism whereby the original will of God was not thwarted by the misfortune or failure of an individual on the one hand or by the greed of speculation on the other. Indeed, if Yahweh was the ultimate owner of the land and it was impossible to buy or sell it, then land could not become a commodity, an object of individual greed.[1] Thus, the very fact that Yahweh owned the land called for a distribution of the land that reflected the divine purpose for the people, namely, a people who had access to the means of survival so that they were dependent upon God alone and not upon the whim of a few wealthy humans.

An Expression of Literal Law?

Ginzberg asserts that the explanation of fixing prices to the proximity of the jubilee shows that the author did not understand the natural economic responses to the legislation.[2] Two assumptions underlie this comment. First, the literal execution of the jubilee legislation would be economically disastrous, thus the jubilee must be considered impractical. Secondly, the authors of the jubilee legislation intended it to be executed literally. Regarding the first assumption, there is little debate; although land reform in general often leads to improved food production,[3] a periodic, universal reform as described by the jubilee laws would cripple a society's economy. However, the second assumption is not self-evident. If the authors intended the jubilee to be executed literally, were they so economically naive that they were unaware of its effects, or did they not care about those effects? The origins of the earlier strata of Leviticus 25 are not clear enough to answer this question about them, but the priests were a part of the ruling class in Jerusalem, involved in financial matters of temple, and they were part of the intelligentsia of a nation in exile in a very advanced empire. It is difficult to believe they could not have foreseen the economic stumbling blocks of the jubilee. On the other hand, if

---

1. Wildberger, 'Israel und sein Land', p. 414.
2. Ginzberg, 'Biblical Economics', p. 385.
3. See R. Berry and W.R. Cline, *Agrarian Structure and Productivity in Developing Countries* (Baltimore: Johns Hopkins University Press, 1979); Dorner, 'Land Tenure Institutions'; A.Y.C. Koo, *Land Market Distortion and Tenure Reform* (Ames: Iowa State University Press, 1982); and D. Warringer, *Land Reform in Principle and Practice* (Oxford: Clarendon Press, 1969).

they were truly concerned with justice, they would have been unable to ignore such consequences and enact the jubilee laws in spite of its negative effects.

But why would the priests include the jubilee legislation in their own legal code if they had not intended actual compliance? As has already been noted, the inclusion of the jubilee in the Priestly Code may have been an attempt to aid the returning exiles in regaining the land they were forced to abandon. In so far as this is a part of the intent of the jubilee, the priests would have hoped for some initial compliance with the laws. It must also be said that the priests did not feel themselves free to discard inconvenient traditions arbitrarily. If the priests believed a tradition was a valid part of orthodox Yahwism, they found ways to adapt it to their own context. They saw the jubilee as a genuine expression of Yahwistic principles (that also could aid the returning exiles); therefore, they passed it along with highly cultic and theological overtones added to it. The priests did not spiritualize the law so much that it became a mere abstraction; land was to be distributed relatively equally among the people and maintained in that way. However, the jubilee was seen as a catalyst to that process, not the process itself; it was a signal to the people, leading them toward a proper relationship with the land.

Chapter 8

THE DOCUMENTARY MEANING

Mannheim states, 'What is "characteristic" in the documentary sense may again be ascertained from the way in which the subject matter is selected and represented, and from the way in which the medium is shaped'.[1] As we examine the documentary meaning, the meaning that lies at a deeper level than the surface objective meaning or the intent of the author, we will discover what aspects of the jubilee caused it to be selected (and not some other tradition) to be the normative land tenure legislation in the Priestly Code, how the priestly formation of that tradition adds to its meaning, how a comparison/contrast with an alternative view (Ezekiel's) further defines the jubilee and what implications lie within the central notion of the divine ownership of the land. One can note that the objective and expressive meanings contribute to the documentary meaning in a dialectical relationship among the three. It will be recognized that many of these converge and reinforce one another.

Clues from the Selected Tradition

One of the most obvious aspects of the jubilee is its apparent 'anti-latifundism'. For the growth of large estates to occur, there must be little or no restraint on the ability of individuals to buy land permanently and bequeath it to successive generations. The existence of a periodic reform as described by the jubilee clearly prevents any such growth. If an individual has prospered and is able to 'buy' the land of a neighbor, the jubilee sets a limit on the existence of the extended farm; the joining of small farms into larger estates can exist no longer than fifty years. Whether the jubilee was ever observed or any of those responsible for its existence (including the priests) ever intended its literal observance has no effect on the anti-latifundism displayed in

1. Mannheim, 'The Interpretation of *Weltanschauung*', p. 56.

the fact of the jubilee's existence. Thus, part of the meaning of the jubilee is that individuals ought not be able to accumulate large tracts of land for their exclusive benefit.

A second aspect of the jubilee tradition is the way in which it attaches the people to the land. The jubilee is not a general notion of egalitarianism, but it declares that *this* person, who is a member of *this* family, has a right to occupy and reap the produce from *this* land. The very specificity of the attachment reinforces the urgency of the proper distribution of the land. A declaration that 'all people ought to have an equal share in the land' is so abstract that one can assent to it easily but never attempt any implementation of it. However, the concrete pairing of this person with that land demands a more reflective and conscientious response. In addition, this concrete attachment binds persons to the land in a way that implies the importance of the land for the people —people and land belong together. Again, the literal observance of the jubilee is not essential to this meaning; the very existence of this concrete attachment between people and land expresses the deeply held beliefs about the land.

A third aspect of the jubilee tradition is its focus on the economic viability of individuals (and presumably their families). This is not to claim for the jubilee an individualism similar to that found in the modern Western world, but the jubilee does not abandon the individual to the general welfare of the corporate body. Each individual family is an important economic unit that ought to have its integrity as a viable body maintained. At this point, the attachment to the land takes on greater significance. In an agrarian society, the most important means of survival is access to land on which to live and grow food; without land one is dependent on the ability to sell one's labor and another's willingness to buy it. (This is also true in an industrialized society although jobs tend to be more plentiful and less seasonal than in an agrarian society.) Since the jubilee attempts to guard every individual family's right to their own land, it ensures the possibility that each family can maintain its economic integrity and remain independently viable.

Counteracting any tendency toward a 'rugged individualism' characteristic of contemporary America is the fourth aspect of the jubilee tradition—familial solidarity. The laws calling for the redemption of land or person declare that people are responsible for the basic welfare of members of their family. Again, the specificity of the regulations, describing which family members are responsible for the redemption, moves the concept of family solidarity from the realm of abstraction (a 'nice idea') to that of concrete action expressing the principle of communal responsibility. The jubilee does include broader and more general admonitions for all Israelites to protect the dignity of all other Israelites—poor Israelites are not to be charged interest on loans, and Israelites are not to be sold as slaves but hired as free laborers and treated well. All of this is stated without a word of judgment concerning the individual in poverty. Whether that person became poor because of crop failure, financial mistakes, imprudence, incompetence or laziness, the community is responsible for keeping that person from falling into a state of abject poverty and the indignity of slavery.

Clues from the Priestly Intent

The priests were self-conscious in their expression of the theological nature of the land tenure issue, but the belief that land tenure was a matter of divine concern was a deep part of the priestly world-view. For the priests, Yahweh was the sovereign of all the world and all matters within the world, and they used the jubilee to indicate that this was also the case with land ownership; therefore, the jubilee as we have it before us denies the compartmentalization of the world. The jubilee repudiates the human tendency to divide sacred and profane realms within life so that parts of a person's or society's existence are matters of indifference to the deity. While economic systems are often legitimated by a community's religion, in practice the economy is allowed to progress independently from religious considerations. The jubilee declares that what some consider 'private' transactions do fall under the rule of God. In particular, persons' access to the means of survival—land—is watched over by God, and the maintenance of proper access for everyone is a religious obligation, not a matter of social choice or even economic expediency.

The priests also added meaning to the jubilee by giving special authority to the old traditions—particularly those associated with Moses. As stated above, the priests believed that the traditions handed down by the ancestors were proper and normative and that it was the people's obligation to fulfill the ancestors' intent rather than repeat their failure. Now the jubilee carries the message that, within the traditions society has held for many generations, there exist values that remain normative for the society regardless of previous compliance. This implies that a community need not rely on the extraordinary brilliance of its intelligentsia or special divine revelation for its knowledge of right and wrong; that knowledge is a part of the community's traditional wisdom and need only be carried out as originally intended. In the case of land tenure, traditional wisdom has dictated that a just share of the land (and its blessings) is a right of every family in the community; therefore, the jubilee seeks to provide a means of implementing that tradition and fulfilling the ideals handed down from the predecessors.

Finally, the priests added the sense that proper land distribution was integral to an orderly world. The jubilee's adoption into the Priestly Code marks it as a crucial component of the cosmic order which must be maintained to avoid chaos, of which the exile was a glimpse. In different societies, different issues take on cosmic significance, for example, the shape of one's house or at what age one must marry. The jubilee declares that the way the land is distributed can make the difference between prosperity and chaos, for to allow the land to become permanently alienated from the family to which it was allotted is to allow the intended order willed by God to disintegrate. Not only is the divine justice offended, the very world created by God unravels, allowing people who are intended to be the free servants of God to become encumbered by debt and dependence. Ultimately, an unequal distribution of land among the people is not only a matter of injustice, it threatens the survival of the whole community by bringing about the destruction of the framework upon which life itself can continue to exist.

Clues from a Comparison with Ezekiel

The jubilee as we now have it occupies a 'middle ground' between practical regulation for everyday existence and idealistic vision of a world that does not exist. This is more easily seen by comparing the land tenure proposed by the jubilee with that proposed by Ezek. 47.13–49.29. The jubilee describes a society that does not exist but functions according to the divine rules of justice, as does Ezekiel's vision. The land is perceived in ways that do not correspond with actual practice, that is, the jubilee declares that the land actually belongs to God, while society continues to function as if land were owned by individual humans. The call for a periodic, universal land reform is a utopian ideal which could not be carried out in the world as it actually exists. In all these ways, the jubilee resembles Ezekiel in that it envisions a new society which conforms to the priestly world-view in ways that the actual world does not.

On the other hand, the jubilee attempts to place this 'utopia' within the boundaries of the real world. Unlike Ezekiel, the land described by the jubilee is not supernaturally fertile (cf. Ezek. 47.1-12) nor is it distributed to an ideal nation which no longer exists (that is, all twelve tribes). The very existence of the jubilee laws presupposes the reality of the tendency toward latifundism and the real spiral of debt and dependency in which small landowners can find themselves. In contrast, Ezekiel seems to assume that once a proper distribution of the land has been executed, inequalities in the new age will not arise—a redistribution will not be necessary. The jubilee acknowledges the realities of this world and then posits a method whereby a society based on divine laws can exist, a society not of 'another place and time' but of this world. Whereas Ezekiel looks to direct divine intervention to inaugurate a new age in which the defects of the present world no longer exist, the jubilee believes that a righteous society is possible to construct here and now. With the proper regulations, the defects of the present world can be corrected and the people can experience true peace and justice.

Implications of Divine Ownership of the Land

The cornerstone of the jubilee is found in v. 23, 'The land shall not be sold in perpetuity, for the land is mine'. The belief in the divine ownership of the land carries with it certain implications, and whether intended by the priests or not, these implications are now a part of the meaning of the jubilee. The first implication is that the land is holy. As long as distinction is made between the sacred and the profane, whatever belongs to God will be considered sacred, set apart from the normal activities of everyday living. For most of what is called sacred —whether objects, places, persons or times—this means an end to all intercourse between that which is consecrated and 'ordinary' objects, places, persons or times. The temple precinct was a holy place and could not be used for everyday purposes. If all the cultivated land of Israel is holy, the sense of holiness must be somewhat different since the prohibition of normal use of this land would mean death. In the case of the land, its sacredness means that it is to function to fulfill the purposes of God exclusively. This leads to the other implications of divine ownership of the land.

If the land is to be used exclusively for God's purposes, it may not be used to further the economic interests of any persons or class of persons. The land may not become a commodity to be bought and sold on speculation in order to enrich a few wealthy individuals. One might even go further and ask whether using the land exclusively for cash crops is a profanation of the divine will. If one's plot of land produces more than is needed, ought the surplus be given to the poor? Obviously, one could go quite far in limiting the uses of the land because of its holy nature, but the jubilee does not set such limits. Divine ownership itself sets the basic limit; one cannot buy or sell what one does not own; therefore, literal transfers of land are impossible, thus the accumulation of large estates is impossible. God may grant the blessing of wealth, but it will not be in the form of latifundia. If the land is holy, then its use ought to conform to God's nature and intent. Part of God's intent for the people is to live in peace, the means of survival being secure from all threats.

Since in an agrarian society, land is the basic ingredient in survival, the land ought to provide the means for life. Augmenting the prohibitions against certain uses of the land, this gives us a notion of prescriptions for certain uses. The land and its produce are meant to secure for people the means to live independently and free from the fear of poverty. Negatively, this excludes using land to wield power over others or to produce the means of death. The purpose of the holy is to enhance life, and using the holy to the detriment of life is a profanation of the holy and invites the revocation of its blessings. Therefore, the divine ownership of the land calls for the proper use of the land, the use that establishes the foundation for the survival of the people.

Because Yahweh is a God of justice, Yahweh's land ought to be used justly. The gift of the land was intended for all the people, not just a select few, and the land ought to remain relatively equally distributed among the people. Since the land is the foundation for the means of survival, access to the land is not to be denied to anyone, but everyone is to have a fair share in the divine gift. As was noted earlier, the jubilee does not take this as a call for communal ownership in which the welfare of the individual is subsumed under the welfare of the group as a whole; rather every person is guaranteed access to that which can ensure independent survival. The right to the blessing of God's land is an inalienable right. In fact, the denial of that right, the exclusion of some from their access to the land, could bring about a chaos in which no one could enjoy the fruit of the land. Thus, God's land, the holy land, is a gift to all persons meant to provide the means for an independent existence.

CONCLUSION

Some common features and trends emerge among the ancient Near Eastern land tenure systems. These societies recognized the state's right to rectify what was judged to be unjust distributions of land (apparently caused by the debt of small landowners), distinguished between ownership and right to usufruct (allowing a landowner to gain liquid assets from equity in the land without selling the land permanently), presupposed the inalienability of the land beyond the family and limited the absolute right of individuals to buy or sell land. There was also a tension in the development of land tenure. On the one hand, there was a centralization of control of the land from smaller units (families or tribes) to the monarchy. On the other hand, there was the increase in the rights of private owners to dispose of their land. These same features and this same ambiguous development can be seen in the history of Israel, and as Israel became more complex, the traditions concerning land tenure grew to respond to the changing conditions. More importantly, those traditions took on theological warrants, claiming divine authority for the kind of equitable distribution of the land that was presupposed by early Israel. The development culminated during the exile when the priests were forced to recreate a society that would conform to the will of Yahweh and thus prosper in the restored homeland.

The main body of this analysis indicated that the exile was a period of traumatic upheaval when the world that had been Israel's security came crashing down with the fall of Jerusalem. During this period, several groups sought to explain the catastrophe in terms of a traditional (with some modifications) Yahwistic understanding of the universe; among these groups were a mainline priesthood and an Ezekielian school. As Babylonia began to weaken and Cyrus appeared as a potential liberator, these groups turned their attention to the formation of a new society based on a particular world-view. When the land tenure system proposed by the mainline priests (the jubilee) was compared with that of the Ezekielian school, it was noted that the mainline priests explicitly founded their system on the traditions of the past, declaring a legitimacy for the social system as it existed. Rather than looking for an eschatological new age when land could be distributed equally once for all time, the mainline priests envisioned a system in the present world that was 'self-correcting', constantly readjusting land distribution in accordance with the divine will.

As I analyzed the levels of meaning within the jubilee, the moral world-view upon which it is built became clearer. At the level of objective meaning it was discovered that the jubilee was a counter to the Canaanite land tenure system which considered land a commodity that could be bought and sold for the purpose of gaining profit. The jubilee declared that agricultural land—land that formed the basis of a family's survival—could not be a commodity, but was inalienably granted to a *particular* family, recognizing the significance of this small social unit independent from the community as a whole. At the level of expressive meaning, it was clear that the intent of the priests was not a simple matter. While there was some intent to maintain power for themselves and to regain land for them and the other returning exiles, they also had a sincere interest in the formation of a just and stable society. They used the old traditions to express their authority and legitimate the society they were proposing. The theological warrants they added to the jubilee legislation provided divine sanction, but they did not confine their vision to an eschatological utopia which had no relation to the world of everyday existence. Finally, the documentary meaning led to the conclusion that the basis of the jubilee is the notion of the divine ownership of the land, which leads to the goal of this study.

The Jubilee as a Moral World-View: Descriptive and Normative

As has been stated before, any world-view combines the 'ought' with the 'is' of a society, and that is also the case with the jubilee. The very nature of the land reform proposed by the jubilee presupposes the economic realities of the ancient Near East. There is an implicit recognition that, for whatever reason, some people prosper in their endeavors while others do not.[1] For example, climatic conditions can

---

1.   Many parts of the Hebrew Bible link prosperity with one's moral character, e.g. Deuteronomy and Proverbs. On the other hand, the tradition recognizes many

ruin persons who farm in certain terrain or grow certain crops. When these facts are combined with the human search for wealth, there seems to be an inevitable tendency toward the accumulation of land in the hands of those who are economically shrewd, politically powerful or lucky. In any case, the jubilee does not retreat to an eschatological age or a utopian society, rather it seeks to insinuate itself in the very existence of the real world.

Yet the jubilee seems also to express the notion that the real world must be understood by a reality that may not be immediately apparent to the casual observer. To the casual observer, the real world may appear to allow, even encourage latifundism. The fact that the world does not seem to recognize the 'true reality' presupposed by the jubilee makes the literal observance of the jubilee laws impractical. That the priests probably realized the impracticality of the jubilee does not imply that it should be regarded as utopian; the priests were still seeking to build a society based on the traditional values in the present world. The jubilee may be an ideal system which displays the existence of a divinely willed world that has not yet been actualized because of human failure to recognize its reality. We *ought* to actualize what really *is*.

Using the tools of the sociology of knowledge has contributed to these conclusions concerning the jubilee in three ways. First, the sociology of knowledge discloses the reasons why certain traditions concerning land tenure were adopted by later generations to express a particular world-view and why those traditions developed into the jubilee as it now appears in Leviticus 25. The presence of ancient traditions that had long been an integral ingredient in the Israelite culture lends a sense of stability to the legal code constructed by the priests. In addition, old traditions heighten the sense that the priests are speaking of the 'real' world, not a utopia. However, these particular traditions were selected because they contained within them the concept of the divine ownership of the land—a concept that was central to the world-view driving the priests' work. These traditions were adapted into the jubilee legislation because the jubilee concept met the political and economic needs of the priests and the other returning exiles.

Secondly, the sociology of knowledge indicates the close correspondence between a group's understanding of reality in the world (the

exceptions, e.g., Naboth and Nabal.

'is') and its moral structure (the 'ought'). This insight helps us understand how the jubilee can relate to the real world and be an ideal law at the same time—how it can be descriptive and normative simultaneously. Without this connection between the 'is' and the 'ought', scholars have struggled needlessly with the erroneous belief that either the jubilee was literal law or it was utopian. Finally, the sociology of knowledge reveals the dialectic relationship between the three levels of meaning present in a social phenomenon. Too many have sought to discover the meaning of a text in either the author's intent or the expression of the text itself. This study has demonstrated that the full meaning of the text must be understood as a result of the interaction of several levels of meaning.

Of course, many variations of the jubilee and alternative systems of land tenure might have met those needs, but this study has shown how and why the jubilee accomplished the Israelite priests' goals in the exilic period. While the sociology of knowledge is not intended to replace any of the other exegetical tools of the biblical scholar, it builds upon the other methods to increase the interpreter's effectiveness in comprehending the rich meaning of these ancient texts. The analysis also provided a method by which the text might yield deep meanings which could be appropriated by modern society. After all, the twentieth-century industrial world shares little with preindustrial ancient Palestine; therefore, the agrarian interests of the Judean priests could hardly be adopted by modern society. Yet we may share much with the priests' deepest convictions concerning a community's moral imperative toward its economically vulnerable members. Perhaps as we attain new insights into the Hebrew Bible, specialists in other fields—ethics, for example—will be able to apply these venerable truths to a world that seems always in need of assistance.

Appendix

The Literary Strata of Leviticus 25

The jubilee legislation went through several stages of development. This is an attempt to provide an overview of that development, showing how these laws were adapted, explained and warranted by succeeding generations. The first level was a corpus of 'debt-sale laws', which regulated the redemption or release of property or persons who were sold because of debt. This level is indicated in uppercase letters. The debt-sale laws were augmented slightly to expand upon those who could serve as redeemers and to exclude property within walled cities. These additions are indicated in normal type. An early exilic redactor expanded upon the meaning of the jubilee and added some theological warrant to the laws. This level is indicated in boldface type. Later in the exile, priestly editors defined the jubilee further and expanded upon the religious warrants. Their sections are in italics. Later priestly editors made a few minor adjustments, and they are within brackets.

(8) You will count for yourself seven sabbaths of years, seven years seven times, so the length of the seven sabbaths of years will be forty-nine years. (9) Then you will send about the sounding trumpet in the seventh month, on the tenth of the month, [on Yom Kippur]. *You will send about a trumpet in all your land. (10) You will consecrate the fiftieth year, and you will proclaim release in the land to all its inhabitants. It will be a jubilee for you. Each of you will return to his allotted land and each will return to his family. (11) The fiftieth year will be a jubilee for you; you will not sow, and you will not reap what grows spontaneously, and you will not gather from the uncut vines. (12) For it is a jubilee; it is holy to you. You will eat its produce from the field.* **(13) In this year of the jubilee, each of you will return to his allotted land.** (14) IF YOU SELL SOMETHING TO YOUR NEIGHBOR OR BUY FROM YOUR NEIGHBOR, EACH OF YOU WILL NOT WRONG HIS BROTHER. **(15) In accordance with the number of years after the jubilee, you will buy from your neighbor; in accordance with the number of years of crops he is selling to you. (16) If there are many years, you will decrease its price because it is the number of crops he is selling to you. (17) Each of you will not wrong his neighbor, but you will fear your God.** *For I am Yahweh your God.*

(18) You will perform my statutes and you will keep my ordinances; you will do them and dwell securely on the land. (19) The land will give its fruit, and you will eat to your satisfaction and dwell securely upon it. (20) [If you say, 'What will we eat in the seventh year since we cannot sow nor gather our produce', (21) I will command my blessing for you on the sixth year. It will make produce for three years. (22) You will sow in the eighth year and eat from the old produce until the ninth year— i.e., until its produce comes, you will eat the old.] *(23) The land will not be sold without right of redemption for the land is mine, and you are resident aliens and sojourners with me. (24) In all the land you possess, you will give redemption to the land.*

(25) IF YOUR BROTHER BECOMES IMPOVERISHED AND SELLS SOME OF HIS ALLOTTED LAND, HIS NEAREST REDEEMER WILL GO AND REDEEM WHAT HIS BROTHER SOLD.(26) IF A PERSON WHO DOES NOT HAVE A REDEEMER PROSPERS AND FINDS SUFFICIENT MEANS TO REDEEM IT, (27) HE WILL RECKON THE YEARS SINCE THE SALE AND REPAY THE OVERPAYMENT TO THE ONE TO WHOM HE SOLD IT, THEN RETURN TO HIS ALLOTTED LAND.(28) BUT IF THERE IS NOT SUFFICIENT MEANS FOUND TO RETRIEVE IT, WHAT HE SOLD WILL BELONG TO THE ONE WHO BOUGHT IT **until the year of the jubilee;** HE WILL GO OUT IN THE JUBILEE AND RETURN TO HIS ALLOTTED LAND. (29) IF A PERSON SELLS A DWELLING HOUSE IN A WALLED CITY, IT MAY BE REDEEMED FOR AN ENTIRE YEAR AFTER ITS SALE—ALL THAT TIME IT MAY BE REDEEMED. (30) BUT IF IT IS NOT REDEEMED BEFORE A FULL YEAR HAS BEEN COMPLETED, THE HOUSE WHICH IS IN THE WALLED CITY WILL BE ESTABLISHED WITHOUT RIGHT OF REDEMPTION TO THE ONE WHO BOUGHT IT AND TO SUCCEEDING GENERATIONS; IT WILL NOT GO OUT IN THE JUBILEE. (31) BUT HOUSES OF VILLAGES THAT HAVE NO SURROUNDING WALL WILL BE RECKONED ALONG WITH THE CULTIVATED LAND; IT WILL HAVE REDEMPTION, AND IT WILL GO OUT IN THE JUBILEE. (32) regarding the cities of the levites, the houses of the cities of their allotted possession, the levites have a perpetual right of redemption. (33) If one of the Levites does not exercise his right of redemption, the house in the city of his allotted possession will go out in the jubilee because the houses of the cities of the Levites are their allotted possession among the Israelites. (34) The open fields of their cities will not be sold because it is their permanent allotted possession.

(35) IF YOUR BROTHER BECOMES IMPOVERISHED, AND HE CANNOT SURVIVE WITH YOU, YOU WILL MAINTAIN HIM; AS A RESIDENT ALIEN OR A SOJOURNER, (36) HE WILL LIVE WITH YOU. YOU WILL NOT TAKE INTEREST OR INCREASE FROM HIM. **You will fear your God and your brother will live with you. (37) You will not give your money at interest, and you will not give your food with increase.** (38) *I am Yahweh your God who brought you out of the land of Egypt to give you the land of Canaan and to be your God.*

(39) IF YOUR BROTHER WITH YOU BECOMES IMPOVERISHED, AND HE IS SOLD TO YOU, YOU WILL NOT MAKE HIM SERVE AS A SLAVE. (40) AS A HIRED SERVANT OR A SOJOURNER, HE WILL LIVE WITH YOU **until the year of the jubilee he will serve you. (41) Then he will go out from you—he and his children with him. He will return to his family, and he will return to the allotted land of his ancestors.** (42) *For they are my servants whom I brought out of the land of Egypt; they will not be sold at a slave auction.* (43) **You will not rule them harshly, but you will fear your God. (44) Regarding your male and female slaves that belong to you,** *you will buy male and female slaves from the resident aliens around you. (45) Also you may buy from the children of the sojourners (who are aliens among you) and from their families who are among you, whom they bore in your land. They will become your possession. (46) You will bequeath them to your children after you as a possession; you may enslave them permanently. But as for your brothers, the Israelites,* **each of you will not rule his brother harshly.**

(47) IF A RESIDENT ALIEN OR A SOJOURNER WITH YOU BECOMES WEALTHY WHILE YOUR BROTHER WITH YOU BECOMES IMPOVERISHED AND IS SOLD TO A RESIDENT ALIEN OR SOJOURNER WITH YOU or to a member of a resident alien's family, (48) after he is sold, he will have redemption; ONE OF HIS BROTHERS WILL REDEEM HIM, (49) or his uncle or cousin will redeem him, or a close relative in his family will redeem him, or (if he prospers) he will redeem himself. (50) **He will reckon with the one who bought him from the year of his purchase until the year of the jubilee. The cost of his purchase will be in accordance with the**

number of years, commensurate with the time of a hired servant with him. (51) If there are still many years, in accordance with them, he will repay his redemption price from the cost of his purchase. (52) If a few years remain until the year of the jubilee, he will reckon with him; in accordance with his years, he will repay his redemption price. (53) HE WILL BE WITH HIM LIKE A SERVANT HIRED YEAR BY YEAR. HE WILL NOT RULE HIM HARSHLY IN YOUR SIGHT (54) But if he is not redeemed by these means, he will go out in the year of the jubilee—he and his children with him.

(55) *For the Israelites are my slaves—they are my slaves whom I brought out from the land of Egypt. I am Yahweh your God.*

Selected Bibliography

Ackroyd, P., *Exile and Restoration* (OTL; Philadelphia: Westminster Press, 1968).

Allan, N., 'The Identity of the Jerusalem Priesthood during the Exile', *HeyJ* 23 (1982), pp. 259-69.

Alt, A., 'The Origins of Israelite Law', in *Essays on Old Testament History and Religion* (trans. R.A. Wilson; Garden City, NY: Doubleday, 1967), pp. 103-71.

Bailey, A.M., and J.R. Llobera, 'The Asiatic Mode of Production: Sources and Formation of the Concept', in *The Asiatic Mode of Production: Science and Politics* (London: Routledge & Kegan Paul, 1981), pp. 13-45.

Baltzer, K., 'Naboths Weinberg (1. Kön. 21): Der Konflict zwischen israelitischem und kanaanäischem Bodenrecht', *Wort und Dienst* 8 (1965), pp. 73-88.

Barton, J., 'Understanding Old Testament Ethics', *JSOT* 9 (1978), pp. 43-64.

Ben-Barek, Z., 'Meribaal and the System of Land Grants in Ancient Israel', *Bib* 62 (1981), pp. 73-91.

Berger, P.L., *The Sacred Canopy: Elements of a Sociological Theory of Religion* (Garden City, NY: Doubleday, 1967; Anchor Books, 1969).

Berger, P.L., and T. Luckmann, *The Social Construction of Reality: A Treatise in the Sociology of Knowledge* (Garden City, NY: Doubleday, 1966).

Berry, R.A., and W.R. Cline, *Agrarian Structure and Productivity in Developing Countries* (Baltimore: Johns Hopkins University Press, 1979).

Bess, S.H., 'Systems of Land Tenure in Ancient Israel' (dissertation, University of Michigan, 1963).

Blenkinsopp, J., *A History of Prophecy in Israel* (Philadelphia: Westminster Press, 1983).

Brueggemann, W., 'The Kerygma of the Priestly Writers', in W. Brueggemann and H.W. Wolff (eds.), *The Vitality of Old Testament Traditions* (Atlanta: John Knox, 1975), pp. 101-13.

—*The Land* (Overtures to Biblical Theology; Philadelphia: Fortress Press, 1977).

—'Reflections on Biblical Understandings of Property', *International Review of Mission* 64 (1974), pp. 354-61.

—'Trajectories in Old Testament Literature and the Sociology of Ancient Israel', in N.K Gottwald (ed.), *The Bible and Liberation: Political and Social Hermeneutics* (Maryknoll: Orbis Books, 1983).

Bryant, R.W.G., *Land: Private Property, Public Control* (Montreal: Harvest House, 1972).

Burridge, K., *New Heaven, New Earth: A Study of Millenarian Activities* (New York: Schocken Books, 1969).

Clay, R., *The Tenure of Land in Babylonia and Assyria* (University of London Institute of Archaeology, Occasional Paper, 1; London: The Institute, 1938).

Collier, P., 'Malfunctioning of African Rural Factor Markets: Theory and a Kenyan Example', *Oxford Bulletin of Economics and Statistics* 45 (May 1983), pp. 141-72.

Cross, F.M., 'The Priestly Work', in *Canaanite Myth and Hebrew Epic: Essays in the History of the Religion of Israel* (Cambridge: Harvard University Press, 1973).

Davison, J.M., 'The Oikoumene in Ferment: A Cross-Cultural Study of the Sixth Century', in C.D. Evans, W.W. Hallo and J.B. White (eds.), *Scripture in Context: Essays on the Comparative Method* (Pittsburgh Theological Monograph Series, 34; Pittsburgh: Pickwick Press, 1980).

Diepold, P., *Israels Land* (Stuttgart: Kohlhammer, 1972).

Dion, H.-M., 'Yahweh, Dieu de Canaan, et la terre des hommes', *Canadian Journal of Theology* 13 (1967), pp. 233-40.

Dorner, P., 'Land Tenure Institutions', in M.G. Blase (ed.) *Institutions in Agricultural Development* (Ames: Iowa State University Press, 1971), pp. 14-31.

Eichrodt, W., *Ezekiel* (OTL; Philadelphia: Westminster Press, 1970).

—'Faith in Providence and Theodicy in the Old Testament', in J. Crenshaw (ed.), *Theodicy in the Old Testament* (Philadelphia: Fortress Press, 1983), pp. 17-41.

—*Theology of the Old Testament* (trans. J.S. Baker; 2 vols.; Philadelphia: Westminster Press, 1961).

Fager, J., 'Land Tenure and the Biblical Jubilee: A Moral World View' (Ann Arbor, MI: University Microfilms, 1987).

Flanagan, J.W., *David's Social Drama: A Hologram of Israel's Early Iron Age* (The Social World of Biblical Antiquities Series, 7; Sheffield: Almond Press, 1988).

Fohrer, G., *History of Israelite Religion* (trans. D.E. Green; Nashville: Abingdon Press, 1972).

Gamoran, H., 'The Biblical Law against Loans on Interest', *JNES* 30 (1971), pp. 127-34.

Geertz, C., *The Interpretation of Cultures: Selected Essays* (New York: Basic Books, 1973).

Gemser, B., 'Motive Clauses in Old Testament Law', *VTSup* 1 (1953), pp. 50-56.

Gerleman, G., 'Nutrecht und Wohnrecht: Zur Bedeutung von *'ḥzh und nḥlh*', *ZAW* 89 (1977), pp. 313-25.

Gese, H., *Der Verfassungsentwurf des Ezekiel (Kap. 40–48) traditionsgeschichtlich Untersucht* (Beiträge zur historischen Theologie, 25; Tübingen: Mohr, 1957).

Ginzberg, E., 'Studies in the Economics of the Bible', *JQR* 22 (1932), pp. 343-408.

Gnuse, R., 'Jubilee Legislation in Leviticus: Israel's Vision of Social Reform', *BTB* 15 (1985), pp. 43-48.

—*You Shall Not Steal: Community and Property in the Biblical Tradition* (Maryknoll, NY: Orbis Books, 1985).

Gottwald, N.K., 'Early Israel and "The Asiatic Mode of Production" in Canaan' in *SBL Seminar Papers* (Missoula, MT: Scholars Press, 1976), pp. 145-54.

—*The Hebrew Bible: A Socio-Literary Introduction* (Philadelphia: Fortress Press, 1985).

—'Sociological Method in the Study of Ancient Israel', in M.J. Buss (ed.), *Encounters with the Text: Form and History in the Hebrew Bible* (Missoula, MT: Scholars Press, 1979).

—*The Tribes of Yahweh* (Maryknoll, NY: Orbis Books, 1979).

Hanson, P.D., *The Diversity of Scripture: A Theological Interpretation* (Overtures to Biblical Theology, 11; Philadelphia: Fortress Press, 1982).

—*The People Called: The Growth of Community in the Bible* (San Francisco: Harper & Row, 1986).

Haran, M., 'Behind the Scenes of History: Determining the Date of the Priestly Source', *JBL* 100 (1981), pp. 321-33.

—'The Law-Code of Ezekiel XL-XLVIII and its Relation to the Priestly School', *HUCA* 50 (1979), pp. 45-71.

Harrod, H., *The Human Center: Moral Agency in the Social World* (Philadelphia: Fortress Press, 1981).

Henrey, K.H., 'Land Tenure in the Old Testament', *PEQ* 34 (1986), pp. 5-15.

Herion, G.A., 'The Impact of Modern and Social Science Assumptions on the Reconstruction of Israelite History', *JSOT* 34 (1986), pp. 3-33.

Hopkins, D.C. *The Highlands of Canaan: Agricultural Life in the Early Iron Age* (The Social World of Biblical Antiquity Series, 3; Sheffield: Almond Press, 1985).

Horst F., 'Das Eigentum nach dem Alten Testament', in *Gottes Recht* (Munich: Chr. Kaiser Verlag, 1961), pp. 203–21.

Howie, C.G., *The Date and Composition of Ezekiel (JBL* Series, 4; Philadelphia: SBL 1950).

Jirku, A., 'Das israelitische Jobeljahr', in *Von Jerusalem nach Ugarit* (Austria: Akademische Druck-u. Verlagsanstalt, 1966), pp. 319-29.

Klein, R.W., *Israel in Exile: A Theological Interpretation* (Overtures to Biblical Theology; Philadelphia: Fortress Press, 1979).

Knight, D., 'Cosmogonic Traditions and Ethical Order', in R.S. Lovin and F.E. Reynolds (eds.), *Cosmogony and Ethical Order: New Studies in Comparative Ethics* (Chicago: University of Chicago Press, 1985), pp. 133-57.

Koo, A.Y.C., *Land Market Distortion and Tenure Reform* (Ames: Iowa State University Press, 1982).

Kornfeld, W., *Das Buch Leviticus* (Die Welt der Bibel: Kleinkommentare zur Heiligen Schrift; Düsseldorf: Patmos, 1972).

Kuhrt, A., 'The Cyrus Cylinder and Achaemenid Imperial Policy', *JSOT* 25 (1983), pp. 83-97.

Landousies, J., 'Le don de la terre de Palestine', *NRT* 99 (1976), pp. 324-36.

Lang, B., *Monotheism and the Prophetic Minority: An Essay in Biblical History and Sociology* (The Social World of Biblical Antiquity Series, 1; Sheffield: Almond Press, 1983).

Lemche, N.P., '*Andurārum* and *Mišarum:* Comments on the Problem of Social Edicts and their Application in the Ancient Near East', *JNES* 38 (1979), pp. 11-22.

—'The Manumission of Slaves—The Fallow Year—The Sabbatical Year—The Jobel Year', *VT* 26 (1976), pp. 38-59.

Leovy, J.G., and G.M. Taylor, 'Law and Social Development in Israel', *ATR* 39 (1957), pp. 9-24.

Levenson, J.D., *Sinai and Zion: An Entry into the Jewish Bible* (Minneapolis, MN: Winston Press, 1985).

—*Theology of the Program of Restoration of Ezekiel 40–48* (Missoula, MT: Scholars Press, 1976).

Lewy, J., 'The Biblical Institution of Derôr in the Light of Akkadian Documents', *Eretz-Israel* 5 (1958), pp. 21-31.

Lipton, M., 'The Theory of the Optimizing Peasant', *Journal of Development Studies* (January 1968), pp. 327-49.

Loewenstamm, S.E., '*m/trybyt* and *nšk*', *JBL* 88 (1969), pp. 78-80.

Malamat, A., 'Mari and the Bible: Some Patterns of Tribal Organizations and Institutions', *JAOS* 82 (1962), pp. 143-50.

Malina, B.J., 'The Social Sciences and Biblical Interpretation', *Int* 36 (1982), pp. 229-42.

Mannheim, K., *Ideology and Utopia: An Introduction to the Sociology of Knowledge* (trans. L. Wirth and E. Shils; New York: Harcourt Brace Jovanovich, 1936).

—'On the Interpretation of *Weltanschauung*', in P. Kecskemeti (ed.), *Essays on the Sociology of Knowledge* (New York: Oxford University Press, 1952), pp. 33-83.

May, H.G., 'Ezekiel', in *Interpreter's Bible* (Nashville: Abingdon Press, 1956), VI.

Meinhold, A., 'Zur Beziehung Gott, Volk, Land im Jobel-Zusammenhang', *BZ* 29 (1985), pp. 245-61.

Mendenhall, G.E., 'The Hebrew Conquest of Palestine', *BA* 24 (1962), pp. 66-87.

—'Social Organization in Early Israel', in F.M. Cross, W.E. Lemke and P.D. Miller, Jr (eds.), *Magnalia Dei: The Mighty Acts of God* (Garden City, NY: Doubleday 1976), pp. 132-51.

Neufeld, E., *The Hittite Laws* (London: Luzac, 1951).

—'Prohibitions against Loans at Interest in Ancient Hebrew Laws', *HUCA* 26 (1955), pp. 355-412.

—'Socio-Economic Background of Yobel and Š^{e}mitta', *Rivistta degli Studi Orientali* 33 (1958), pp. 53-124.

Newsome, J.D., *By the Waters of Babylon: An Introduction to the History of the Exile* (Atlanta: John Knox, 1979).

North, R., 'The Biblical Jubilee and Social Reform', *Scr* 4 (1951), pp. 323-35.

—'Jobel', *Theologisches Wörterbuch zum Alten Testament* (ed. G. Johannes Botterwick and H. Ringgren; Stuttgart: Kohlhammer, 1982).

—'Maccabean Sabbath Years', *Bib* 34 (1953), pp. 501-15.

—*Sociology of the Biblical Jubilee* (Rome: Pontifical Biblical Institute, 1954).

Noth, M., 'The Laws in the Pentateuch', in *The Laws in the Pentateuch and Other Studies* (London: SCM Press, 1984), pp. 1-107.

—*Leviticus* (OTL; Philadelphia: Westminster Press, 1977).

Oded, B., 'Judah and the Exile', in J.H. Hayes and J.M. Miller (eds.), *Israelite and Judean History* (OTL; Philadelphia: Westminster Press, 1977), pp. 435-88

Patrick, D., *Old Testament Law* (Atlanta: John Knox, 1985).

Pedersen, J., *Israel: Its Life and Culture* (2 vols.; London: Oxford University Press, 1926).

Ploeg, J. van der, 'Studies in Hebrew Law', *CBQ* 13 (1951), pp. 164-71.

Plöger, O., *Theocracy and Eschatology* (trans. S. Rudman; Richmond, VA: John Knox, 1968).

Poggioli, R., 'Naboth's Vineyard or the Pastoral View of the Social Order', *Journal of the History of Ideas* 24 (1963), pp. 3-24.

Porter, J.R., *Leviticus* (CBC; Cambridge: Cambridge University Press, 1976).

Rabinowitz, J.J., 'A Biblical Parallel to a Legal Formula from Ugarit', *VT* 8 (1958), p. 95.

Rad, G. von, *Old Testament Theology* (trans. D.M.G. Stalker; 2 vols.; New York: Harper & Row, 1962-65).

—'The Promised Land and Yahweh's Land in the Hexateuch', in *The Problem of the Hexateuch and Other Essays* (trans. E.W. Trueman Dicken; London: SCM Press, 1984), pp. 79-93.

—*Studies in Deuteronomy* (trans. D. Stalker; Chicago: Henry Regnery, 1953).

Reventlow, H.G., *Das Heiligkeitsgesetz: Formgeschichtlich Untersucht* (Neukirchen: Neukirchener Verlag, 1961).

Ringe, S.H., *Jesus, Liberation, and the Biblical Jubilee: Images for Ethics and Christology* (Overtures to Biblical Theology; Philadelphia: Fortress Press, 1985).

Sawer, M., *Marxism and the Question of the Asiatic Mode of Production* (The Hague: Martinus Nijhoff, 1977).

Schaeffer, H., *Hebrew Tribal Economy and the Jubilee* (Leipzig: Hinrichs, 1922).

Schmid, H.H., *Gerechtigkeit als Weltordnung* (Tübingen: Mohr, 1968).

Schutz, A., and T. Luckmann, *The Structure of the Life-World* (trans. R.M. Zaner and H.T. Engelhardt, Jr; Evanston: Northwestern University Press, 1973).

Selms, A. van, *Year of Jubilee* (IDBSup; Nashville: Abingdon Press, 1976), pp. 496-97.

Sen, A., 'Starvation and Exchange Entitlements: A General Approach and its Application to the Great Bengal Famine', *Cambridge Journal of Economics* (January 1977), pp. 33-59.

Silver, M., *Prophets and Markets: The Political Economy of Ancient Israel* (Social Dimensions of Economics; Boston: Kluwer-Nijhoff Publishing, 1983).

Smith, M., *Palestinian Parties and Politics that Shaped the Old Testament* (New York: Columbia University Press, 1971).

Smith, W.R., *Lectures on the Religion of the Semites* (The Library of Biblical Studies; New York: Ktav, 3rd edn, 1969).

Sonsino, R., *Motive Clauses in Hebrew Law* (SBLDS, 45; Chico, CA: Scholars Press, 1980).

Soss, N.M., 'Old Testament Law and Economic Society', *Journal of the History of Ideas* 34 (1973), pp. 323-44.

Steck, O.H., 'Theological Streams of Tradition', in D.A. Knight (ed.), *Tradition and Theology in the Old Testament* (Philadelphia: Fortress Press, 1977), pp. 183-214.

Talmon, S., and M. Fishbane, 'The Structuring of Biblical Books: Studies in the Book of Ezekiel', *ASTI* 10 (1976), pp. 129-53.

Thomas, D.W., 'The Sixth Century B.C.: A Creative Epoch in the History of Israel', *JSS* 6 (1961), pp. 33-46.

Vaux, R. de, *Ancient Israel* (2 vols.; New York: McGraw-Hill, 1965).

Wacholder, B.Z., 'The Calendar of Sabbatical Cycles during the Second Temple and the Early Rabbinic Period', *HUCA* 44 (1973), pp. 153-96.

Waldow, H.E. von, 'Social Responsibility and Social Structure in Early Israel', *CBQ* 32 (1970), pp. 182-204.

Wallace, A.F.C., 'Revitalization Movements', *American Anthropologist* 58 (1956), pp. 264-81.

Wallis, G., 'Das Jobeljahr-Gesetz, eine Novelle zum Sabbatjahr-Gesetz', *Mitteilungen des Instituts für Orientforschung* 15 (1969), pp. 337-45.

Warringer, D., *Land Reform in Principle and Practice* (Oxford: Clarendon Press, 1969).

Weber, M., *Ancient Judaism* (trans. and ed. H. Gerth and D. Martindale; New York: The Free Press, 1967 [1952]).

Wenham, G.J., *The Book of Leviticus* (Grand Rapids: Eerdmans, 1979).

Westbrook, R., 'Jubilee Laws', *Israel Law Review* 6 (1971), pp. 209-26.

—'Redemption of Land', *Israel Law Review* 6 (1971), pp. 367-75.

Wildberger, H., 'Israel und sein Land', *EvT* 16 (1956), pp. 404-22.

Wilkie, J.M., 'Nabonidus and the Later Jewish Exiles', *JTS*, NS 2 (1951), pp. 36-44.

Wright, C.J.H., *God's People in God's Land: Family, Land, and Property in the Old Testament* (Grand Rapids: Eerdmans, 1990).

Zimmerli, W., *Ezekiel* (2 vols.; Hermeneia; Philadelphia: Fortress Press, 1983).

—'Das "Gnadenjahr des Herrn"', in A. Kuschke and E. Kutsch (eds.), *Archäologie und Altes Testament: Festschrift für Kurt Galling* (Tübingen: Mohr, 1970), pp. 321-22.

—*Old Testament Theology in Outline* (trans. D.E. Green; Edinburgh: T. & T. Clark, 1978).

—*The Old Testament and the World* (Atlanta: John Knox, 1976).

—'Plans for Rebuilding after the Catastrophe of 587', in W. Brueggemann (ed.), *I Am Yahweh* (trans. D.W. Stott; Atlanta: John Knox, 1984).

Ziskind, J.R., 'Petrus Cunaeus on Theocracy, Jubilee and the Latifundia', *JQR* 68 (1978), pp. 235-54.

Index of References

Old Testament

INDEX OF AUTHORS

JOURNAL FOR THE STUDY OF THE OLD TESTAMENT

Supplement Series